HAUN...

HIGHGATE

HAUNTED
HIGHGATE

Della Farrant

The
History
Press

Dedicated to the memory of A.L.B. Farrant,
laid to rest on Mothering Sunday 2014
aged 15 years old.
Always in our hearts.

First published 2014

The History Press
The Mill, Brimscombe Port
Stroud, Gloucestershire, GL5 2QG
www.thehistorypress.co.uk

British Library Cataloguing in Publication Data.
A catalogue record for this book is available from the British Library.

ISBN 978 0 7509 5831 8

Typesetting and origination by The History Press
Printed in Great Britain

CONTENTS

ACKNOWLEDGEMENTS

I am indebted to the following for making this book possible, whether for their encouragement, time and enthusiasm, or their assistance with research material. In no particular order: Alan Murdie, Philip Hutchinson and John Fraser of The Ghost Club; Dave Milner; Redmond McWilliams; The Hornsey Historical Society; Gareth J. Medway; Deborah Meredith; Neil Arnold; Paul Screeton; Paul Adams; David Saunderson; Lorcan Maguire; Dr Chris Laoutaris; the editorial team at the *Ham & High*; Fr Pat Fitzgerald; Dr Sarah Wise; Dr Ian Dungavell; Michael Hammerson; Charles Walker; Brian Sutcliffe; Dee Monique; Jon Randall and Maria Malo; Kenny Frewin; Becky Beach; Gareth Davies; Reeves Cooke; the team at NLPI; Drew Hartley; Patsy Langley and Ricky Sorenti; Paul Quinn; Glyn Morgan; John Plews; Max Sycamore; Melusine Draco; Ken Rees; Alys Tomlinson; the late Mhairi Kent; Joao Ferreira; Steve Genier; Vinnie De Moraes Luz; John Goodchild; Brian Bourne; Mum, Dad, Neil and Pete; Andy Antoniou; S.P.; and last but not least my ever-patient husband David, access to whose invaluable archives enabled me to revisit many of his early investigations.

I would also like to extend thanks to all the witnesses cited in the following pages, of whom there are far too many names to mention here, for their generosity in sharing their personal experiences.

FOREWORD

For many years members of the Ghost Club have taken an interest in the ghost stories that have circulated concerning Highgate Cemetery, the vast Victorian necropolis that opened in 1839. Indeed, one of my predecessors as chairman of the club, Tom Perrott (1921–2013), lived nearby for many years at Muswell Hill and thus was conveniently placed to monitor how rumours of sinister apparitions appearing in the Victorian cemetery expanded to the point that even a vampire was claimed to be prowling the area.

Tom Perrott was not alone in being surprised and sceptical concerning such stories, the general view amongst most British ghost hunters being that cemeteries and graveyards are largely *unhaunted*. Despite popular associations in folklore and fiction, very few people have been known to die in graveyards, and as veteran investigator Andrew Green (1927–2004) observed in *Ghost Hunting: A Practical Guide* (1973), 'because the association does exist in people's minds, quite normal occurrences on the site, or in the new buildings constructed on it, are often assumed to be paranormal phenomena'.

What happened at Highgate, however, could hardly be described as normal. Wild rumours of menacing phantoms and vampires flourished, fuelled by excited media coverage and claims of occult rituals practised after dark. Following one TV broadcast in March 1970, hundreds of people spontaneously descended upon Highgate Cemetery in a mass ghost/vampire hunt worthy of the ending of a horror film, until the police restored order. For some it was a great irony that the arch-prophet of materialist philosophy Karl Marx, who had once written of the 'vampire of capitalism', should have his tomb at a place where so many supernatural stories accumulated.

With many conflicting versions and accounts of these events in circulation, what has long been needed is a serious book sifting out, so far as possible, facts from fantasy concerning ghost experiences in Highgate. In this fascinating book, Della Farrant succeeds admirably in this delicate and complex task.

Writing from the unique perspective of being the wife of a key participant in some of the events described, she has also embarked upon extensive and independent research, tracing original sources and seeking out witnesses and corroborative evidence. Whilst part of the job of a serious writer on ghosts is to quash exaggerated rumours, at the same time the opportunity to record contemporary beliefs and experiences should never be missed. Indeed, it must be recognised that folklore and popular stories can sometimes provide clues to the presence of genuine phenomena. As readers will soon realise, not all in this book can be ascribed to imagination or urban myth.

In *Haunted Highgate*, Della Farrant firmly establishes that people do indeed have strange experiences, in no way limited to just the cemetery and its environs. In recording these accounts here, she restores much-needed balance to the study of ghosts in the Highgate district, as well as providing a wealth of fascinating new stories and material for readers to analyse, ponder and enjoy.

Alan Murdie, 2014
Chairman of The Ghost Club

INTRODUCTION

The very name Highgate suggests a place in between two worlds, deriving from the Saxon *haeg* and the Old English *gat*. This 'gap in the hawthorn hedge' has been a place of flux and movement between north and south for over seven centuries, and in the process has evolved from a fledgling hamlet into an affluent suburb. Millions of people have passed through Highgate since 1318, perhaps leaving behind some of their energy – for this ancient and unspoiled area of North London is believed by many to be one of the most haunted locations in the UK.

Advocates of 'ostention theory', including notable researchers such as American folklorist Professor Bill Ellis, have attempted critical overviews of the more overtly sociological aspects of Highgate's haunted history. This school of thought upholds the concept that people who have been primed to expect a specific paranormal experience will often 'have' one, and that through the power of auto-suggestion they can erroneously come to believe that they have had a genuine encounter with a supernatural agency. Adherents to such approaches, when analysing some of the more famous reports of psychical activity in Highgate,

often surmise that it was the press which helped *create* the concept of such alleged phenomena in the first place. Whilst researching this book, I have conducted conversations and interviews in person, often in Highgate itself, with countless residents of many decades' incumbency who state the opposite, and it is these villagers past and present to whom I am primarily indebted.

It was in the early 1970s that Highgate's supernatural activity first began to be recorded in earnest in the popular press. The shortage of early written records on the subject, when contrasted with strong oral traditions, suggests that this now gentrified village's notable class divide placed ghosts and superstition firmly in the realm of the semi-rural 'peasant classes'. Until the second half of the twentieth century it was not these people, of course, who were writing books, keeping journals, or being interviewed for newspapers.

Fortunately for us, the appearance and habits of some of the ghosts which still roam Highgate also help tell their own unwritten stories, many of which are recorded in print here for the first time. I hope they approve.

Della Farrant, Highgate, 2014

1

SWAINS LANE:

HIGHGATE'S MOST HAUNTED THOROUGHFARE

Over the last few decades, thousands of books, magazines, broadcasts and websites have immortalised Highgate's haunted reputation, chiefly focusing upon its famous Victorian burial grounds. But while these certainly have their resident ghosts, the sheer scope of the paranormal phenomena associated with Swains Lane itself marks it out as potentially more haunted than both cemeteries combined.

One of Highgate's oldest trade routes, the lane takes its name from the swine which were herded down it towards Spitalfields Market from at least the fourteenth century. Its steep incline, extending some three-quarters of a mile south from Highgate Village, today divides the West and East sections of Highgate Cemetery, and the West Cemetery from Waterlow Park. Like many old drovers' roads it presents a lonely and isolated aspect, an impression which is enhanced by the high fences and thick stone walls which border it on both sides. While the lower end of the lane is marked by a thriving community of houses and shops, the northern ascent is segmented only occasionally by Victorian workers' cottages, the cemeteries' three

gates and chapel, and a handful of architectural experiments devised from the late 1960s. The latter are barely observable, sitting as they do within the walls of the West Cemetery itself. There is little traffic at night, and the heavy silence can swiftly become quite overwhelming for a nocturnal pedestrian.

That Swains Lane's sinister reputation spans at least several centuries is no surprise, for there are scores of murders, suicides and other tragic deaths associated with this small stretch of road. By the 1960s its many eerie cuttings, once plagued by highwaymen and footpads, had long since been closed off and built over. Swains Lane itself now benefited from tarmac and occasional electric street lights – not that these indications of urbanisation presented much comfort to those who had recourse to traverse it after nightfall. There are still no public telephone boxes or street-facing residences in the vicinity, and the knowledge that one is surrounded by the remains of hundreds of thousands of London's dead, now as then does little to assuage a strong sense of foreboding. Granting views into the darkened cemetery, within which shadows seem to dart amongst crumbling tombs, and paths lead into impenetrable blackness, the North Gate especially can take some courage to pass, and even more for the foolhardy ghost hunter determined to pause for a glimpse inside. Indeed, many Highgate residents who grew up in the area remember childhood stories of a bogeyman in Swains Lane who would 'get you' if you ventured down the hill alone after dark. The lane is still generally avoided at night by the majority of locals, if only for reasons of practical safety.

Present-day villagers are certainly not the first generation to be aware of rumours of something supernatural abroad in Highgate. Edmund Hodgson Yates, an author who spent his 1830s childhood in the village, recalled in his memoirs:

> Almost my earliest terror was excited by the narrative of the adventures of 'Spring-Heeled Jack' — a ghost which had been playing up its pranks, springing onto the women and nearly frightening them to death, and the scene of whose adventures some of the narrators, knowing the advantage of local colour, had laid in Highgate.

A strange, satirical tract survives which goes somewhat further, leaving us with the tantalising suggestion that by 1808

at least, the residents of Highgate had acquired the social stigma of being easily frightened, and prone to interpreting mundane events as paranormal. With strong suggestions throughout that it was written as a parody of some earlier event or events, the final chapter of *Gambado on Horsemanship*, a slim volume of equine-related humorous tales, finds the whole village convinced that a 'man, drest much after the manner of the English, but of a fierce and terrifying aspect' replete with a forked tail, is gadding about the village with unnatural speed and ambushing them at night. This intruder concerns the local populace to such a degree that they immediately form various unofficial committees in order to decide what to do about it. After several investigations, including deferring to 'books that treat of Witchcraft; Glanville, and Moore, and Wanley', these 'unfortunate Highgates' are left looking rather silly when 'the Phenomenon of Highgate Hill' turns out to be nothing more than a somewhat dishevelled gentleman whose horse had skidded on the ice. One burning question remains — just what had happened at Highgate to inspire this mockery in the first instance? The joke is somewhat lost on the modern reader, who will never have the first-hand experience of hearing tales from eighteenth-century travellers

and holidaymakers about the superstitious folk of Highgate who, 'all the Water at a stop – all the Gin a-going', were apparently perceived to be prone to bouts of collective hysteria.

We shall revisit another period of 'all the Gin a-going' supernaturally inspired mayhem when we enter the imposing main gates of Highgate Cemetery West and flashback to the extraordinary events of 1970. But for a short time let us tarry in the unnerving and somewhat gothic Swains Lane itself, and relive some encounters with its most famous 'ghost'.

A Top-Hatted Victorian Ghost?

It is in a letter to the *Hampstead & Highgate Express*, better known as the *Ham & High*, penned by a Mr R. Docherty of 69 West Hill, Highgate, in February 1970, that we find what seems to be the first written reference to a hat-sporting entity in Swains Lane. 'There is without doubt a ghost,' writes Mr Docherty:

> Of when and whom he originated I do not know. Many tales are told, however, about a tall man in a hat who walks across Swains Lane and just disappears through a wall into the cemetery. Local superstition also has it that the bells in the old disused chapel inside the cemetery toll mysteriously whenever he walks.

There seems to be a dearth of recorded sightings of this distinctively attired figure in the lane until two decades later. A clear sighting comes from a Declan Walsh. One cold November morning in 1991 at around 6.30 a.m., Declan was walking to work down Swains Lane. He recalls that it was a dark morning, but that the street lamps afforded some light as dawn began to break. As leaves from the cemetery's many sycamore trees crunched under his feet, he saw, moving at a right angle to him a short distance ahead, a tall man:

> dressed in black, Victorian style clothing including a cape and top hat. He walked directly towards the gates. The gates were locked shut but he walked straight through them without altering his stride, nor did he make any sounds. I walked past on the other side and could see no one else present.

The Ghost that Tried to Hitch a Ride

That the entity seemed unaware of Declan's presence was perhaps a blessing. One witness to the top-hatted figure whom this author has personally interviewed, and who claims more than one sighting, remains disturbed by what she saw to this day. In 1996 Deborah Meredith was a newcomer to Highgate. Then single and in her mid-twenties, she quickly found work as a taxi driver, often ferrying punters home from the village's many public houses. Having yet to make friends in the area and working unsociable night shifts, Deborah was unaware of Swains Lane's haunted reputation. This might explain why one night around Christmas time that year she stopped her cab to pick up Highgate's least desirable 'fare'. Deborah's encounter with what she refers to as 'the man in black' occurred as she was returning to Highgate at around four in the morning. As her cab surmounted the upper hump of the lane, she suddenly felt as though its speed had slowed from 30 to less than 5 miles per hour, and attempted to change gear in confusion. Looking back today, Deborah remembers the whole sequence of events as having happened almost in slow motion.

As the summit of the lane eventually came into view some 15 yards on, Deborah distinctly perceived the figure of a tall man, wearing a smart but old-fashioned 'Abraham Lincoln-style outfit', standing motionless in front of the North Gate of Highgate Cemetery. In the glare of the headlights the figure slowly but purposefully raised his right hand towards her in a beckoning fashion. Not knowing what to make of this stranger, Deborah drew level with him and pulled into the small parking bay opposite. As she opened the door on the driver's side, with one foot on the ground and one hand on the steering wheel ready to heave herself out of the cab, she called out to the man, enquiring whether he needed a lift to wherever he was going. In an interview with this author, Deborah recalled:

> Because I was a taxi lady, I thought that he may need to get somewhere, but as I went to open the door and speak to him, things did not seem right, and with no one else around, I had second thoughts and drove off. I felt so guilty driving away, with him looking at me in the rear-view mirror. But then in the blink of an eye he had gone. On returning home it bothered me a lot, that I did not know where he went.

In the seconds during which Deborah shifted her gaze from the rear-view mirror, the figure had vanished. It did so in a part of Swains Lane lined with impossibly high stone walls and no means of exit.

There is logic in the assumption that creatures of the night are likely to bump into each other. Research spanning many years, by a variety of paranormal groups, indicates that employees of the London Underground who oversee the empty tracks and platforms by night have many more encounters with the Tube's paranormal inhabitants than the millions of travellers who swarm into its tunnels each day. As we have seen, whilst the top-hatted figure in Swains Lane has been sighted at various times of day and night, it seems to manifest primarily after sundown and before daybreak proper. Unfortunately for Deborah, her regular route up Swains Lane seems to have increased the likelihood of further encounters, as by her own account she saw the figure on several more occasions, even developing the uneasy sense that he was expecting her. Could it be the case that Deborah's regular journeys up the lane made the entity feel at ease in her presence? On one of these occasions, after glimpsing the figure again standing outside the top gate, Deborah asked her passenger if he had also seen the spectre, but frustratingly he had not. Perhaps he had had one too many at the Archway Tavern and was somewhat desensitised to the lane's brooding man in black!

Over the coming months Deborah became friendly with locals in Highgate Village, and tentatively made enquiries about any ghost stories they knew of. Over drinks in The Flask public house she learned that for many years a tall, solitary man in a distinctive hat had been seen by villagers in various parts of Swains Lane. A legend popular at that time held that a woman he was very much in love with had been buried in the cemetery, and that he was waiting in perpetuity for her to return to him, presumably through the iron gates.

A Nocturnal Encounter in Waterlow Park

Nicholas Palma, a former Metropolitan Police officer now living in Cyprus, contacted this author in 2012 to share his memories of an incident which occurred in nearby Waterlow Park. Formerly constituting the private grounds of Lauderdale House, a Tudor mansion originally built in 1582, the park was gifted to the public as a 'a garden for the gardenless' in 1889 by Sir Sydney Waterlow. Unlike many other well-maintained open spaces in and around the capital, Waterlow Park retains an atmosphere of privacy. Indeed, standing in the shadows of its many statues on a warm summer's day whilst watching the carp, ducks and other wildlife, one can easily forget that this haven is still, technically, a part of modern-day London.

Prior to joining the force and whilst in their mid-twenties, Nick and a friend whom I have been asked to refer to only as 'Xever' were accustomed to spending moonlit evenings in the park. Born and raised in Highgate, both shared a passion for its open spaces and what they considered to be its mystical atmosphere. Since their childhoods the two friends, being of contemplative natures, had regularly climbed over one or other of the park's locked gates to enjoy its peace and tranquillity after dark. One dry autumn evening in 1994, Nick and Xever were slowly completing their regular circuit of the park, chatting sporadically as they meandered. It was a night like any other, although they did notice that the park was mistier than usual for August. Certainly not for the first time, they found themselves heading north-west, with Swains Lane just across the wall to their left. Nick takes up the story:

> It was when we got to the Swains Lane side [that] things got eerie, almost sinister. It seemed to get darker, more shadowy, and I'll never forget Xever bundling me into a bush in sheer terror. That might sound amusing, but it certainly wasn't at the time. Once in the bush I demanded an explanation, and he swore that 15 feet away he saw a tall figure in a long black coat charging towards us. I peeped out of the bush but saw nothing. He did not accept my explanation that it might have been a park keeper or even a policeman (we were, after all, in the park after closing time). When I asked how tall this figure was, Xever said he was much taller than me (I am 6 feet 2 inches). I did not see it, and am cynical by nature, but I fully trust my friend. He is no fantasist or liar, and his terror was very real.

As an interesting aside, Xever also attested that their potential assailant was wearing an unusual hat, something like the stove-pipe style kalimavkions worn by Greek Orthodox priests. In recent years Nick has pondered whether Xever's British Cypriot upbringing could have led him to homogenise an anachronistic top hat into an item of clothing with which he was more familiar. This isolated but clearly impactful incident was to bring to an end Xever's visits to the park, as according to Nick his friend never returned there again. Indeed, Xever's encounter with the figure in black unsettled him to such a degree that he descended into a period of uncharacteristic depression and nervous anxiety. As Nick remembers:

After the event in the park Xever became obsessed with finding out what precisely had happened. He became a virtual recluse, only reading about the paranormal. He got involved with all manner of charlatans in his search for an answer. It took many years for him to let it go, so to speak.

Was this tall and aggressive stranger of human or supernatural origin? And how did Nick not notice such a striking figure? Neither young man heard footsteps disturbing the autumn leaves as the figure approached or departed. Nick and Xever outnumbered it two to one and no weapon was being brandished at them, and yet from the moment the stranger made eye contact with Xever it overwhelmed him with sensations of horror and panic.

Locked Gates Present No Barrier in Cholmeley Park

If the figure which Xever saw that night in 1994 was the same seen by Deborah Meredith that same year, and that seen by Declan Walsh almost opposite the path in the park, then it does seem to have previous form for taking nocturnal jaunts beyond the lane's narrow confines. Doug Cohen remembers a story which his father Sidney would never tire of retelling – and puzzling over. 'I just can't work out how he did it,' Sidney, a staunch disbeliever in the supernatural, would for many years remark with bafflement. One Sunday evening in the beginning of July 1969, Sidney and his wife Esther were returning to their home on Archway Road after meeting friends in The Rose and Crown public house.

The path in Waterlow Park where Nicholas Palma and his friend Xever encountered a tall-hatted figure in 1994.

A modern view of the site of the Cohen's 1969 sighting in Cholmeley Park. (© Dave Milner)

After strolling down Highgate Hill they turned left into Cholmeley Park, a quiet residential street. The couple had just passed the steps to the second block of art deco flats, which are separated from the pavement by a 4- to 5ft-high wall, when they noticed a movement in the road. Both Sidney and Esther watched as a tall, gaunt man wearing a long, black coat and top hat crossed to their side of the street and continued down the pavement, some 20 yards ahead of them. The Cohens immediately ceased their conversation and stared at the strangely dressed man. In the seconds during which they looked away to exchange quizzical glances, he had vanished. As Audrey stayed rooted to the spot, Sidney – perhaps fuelled with a little Dutch courage – raced some 20 yards down the silent street to the first turning on the left. When he reached the gated driveway leading to Furnival House,

an imposing mansion built in 1916, Sidney rattled the padlocks on all three gates, only to discover that they were securely locked and the grounds deserted.

A Hiss in One's Ear on a Warm Summer Night

In 2005 Mr Martin Trent, a resident of the Holly Lodge Estate which borders Highgate Cemetery West at its southern extremity, had a disturbing encounter with a tall, dark figure which still preys upon his mind. The following events occurred around midnight one July or August, towards the end of that sultry and humid summer, as Martin was making his way home from a night out at The Duke's Head in Highgate Village. The route was very familiar to him, as he recalls:

In all that time of walking up and down the lane at various times of the day and dead of night, in all conditions and through every season, I never felt or saw anything amiss. Sure, sometimes on a particularly misty late night in November, it could be a little spooky, wending my way down from the village, past the cemetery gates. But, I had never before sensed anything even remotely approaching a ghost or apparition sighting.

However, on this occasion, as Martin walked down Swains Lane, with Waterlow Park to his left and Highgate Cemetery West to his right, he spotted the tall figure of a man, some 25 yards ahead of him, standing near the East Cemetery gates. Martin recalls that he himself was wearing a T-shirt and shorts due to the insufferable heat, and that as he got nearer, he began to think that this figure looked a bit 'odd'. The stranger was dressed in dark, drab clothing, but what seemed especially peculiar was the fact that he appeared to be wearing a long overcoat – and a stove-pipe hat. As Martin drew closer to the mysterious figure, he began to feel increasingly uneasy; although it appeared to be human, it was entirely motionless, displaying no signs of life whatsoever. As Martin points out, there are often groups of disaffected teenagers hanging around the cemetery gates, at all hours of the day and night. So the fact that he was not alone in the lane on that evening was not particularly surprising. The really strange part, though, was yet to come …

Martin had been walking in the middle of the dimly lit lane, but as he approached the figure he veered to his right, to create as great a distance as possible between them. Strangely, Martin's fear then moderated slightly, and he began to receive the strong impression from the figure that, as he puts it, 'it knew why it was there, and that it had every right to be there'. The figure seemed to him to be completely in tune with its surroundings, and to be strongly conveying this to him. As Martin dropped his gaze to avoid eye contact, the two eventually drew level, some 10 feet of road separating them. It was at this point that Martin was appalled to hear the stranger speak:

I could swear I heard him say to me, 'Good evening to you, sir,' in what sounded at first like a strange accent, but which I later thought just sounded old fashioned. The other peculiarity about his greeting was that it didn't seem to come from his direction as such, but rather seemed to be hissed right next to my ear – which, given the ordinariness of the words, still gave me a jolt. I'm not even sure if the voice was male or female, now. It seemed to be oddly neutral as far as I can remember.

In an interview with this author in 2012, when asked whether he considered replying to the entity's salutation, Martin described the whole experience as giving him a kind of brain fog, akin to being hypnotised. He remembers, with some embarrassment, his thoughts becoming scrambled, and a sense that his whole consciousness had narrowed to that confusing moment in time – which in fact seemed to exist outside of time. To return to Martin's narrative:

I continued past him for about a further 50 yards down the lane and just as I was about to turn right into my road – Oakeshott Avenue – something made me turn round. Looking up the rise from where I was standing, he was now on the other side of the road, nearer to Highgate Cemetery West. From my position, given the camber of the lane, I couldn't see his feet, but the next moment he seemed to glide at a right angle to me clean through the [locked] cemetery gates on the opposite side of the lane and disappear into the East Cemetery.

It is quite possible to recreate Martin's observer/object viewpoint – the dip in the lane between the two sets of gates does indeed make it impossible to see the lower regions of anyone crossing the lane at this point.

I went home and immediately told my wife. She seemed more excited by it than me at the time. We had both had problems with the signals and batteries of our mobile phones during the years we had lived on the Holly Lodge Estate, and found having a bath with a view of the cemetery a bit unnerving, but this was something entirely unprecedented. The whole incident had a delayed effect on me. It was only a few days later, when I was mulling it over in my mind, that it all seemed to come into focus and I realised what an extraordinary 'encounter' I'd had. The bit that kept gnawing away at me, and left me feeling decidedly uncomfortable, was the whispered greeting that seemed to come from right next to me, rather than from the direction where 'he' was standing. That definitely put the frighteners up me. Strangely enough, I feel more unsettled recalling the events now, even with distance and perspective, than I did at the time they actually occurred, and I can't deny I don't have quite the same assuredness walking home down Swains Lane at night any more.

Martin's perception of the entity as 'preternaturally strange' was exacerbated by the unnatural manner in which it crossed the lane, almost, as Martin puts it, as if it were on wheels, with no normal perambulatory motions at all. He also recalls his close-up encounter with the entity, describing its face as gaunt, with high cheekbones. This visage was the figure's only clearly discernible aspect, as the lamplight seemed unable to illuminate the dun appearance of the rest of its form, save for the silhouette of its anachronistic clothing. The face appeared to be that of someone at most in their early thirties, and this surprised him as, for reasons he does not understand, he expected it to appear older.

A Nineteenth-Century Encounter with the Man in Black

Martin's visual, aural and emotional experiences are reminiscent of an anonymous letter published in the *New Zealand Herald* on 21 October 1868. In the letter, an ex-pat, remembering his days living in London some decades previously, describes being followed by a supernatural being whilst walking home down Hampstead Road, 'ever so far up', one extremely icy night approaching Christmastime. Hampstead Road runs north to south in a direct continuation of Swains Lane and Kentish Town Road.

In the 1860s much of this area was still part of the old countrified ascent to Highgate and the Northern Heights. 'In the centre of the road,' the letter attests:

was a man, tall, thin, cadaverous, mysterious, noiseless. The first thought which rushed into my head when I beheld my spectral friend, was 'is he human or superhuman' […] A cold clammy perspiration beaded on my forehead. […] Instinctively I found myself walking on again sharply, hoping that my companion would, by dint of exertion on my part, soon be left behind. As I quickened my pace, my spectral friend quickened his also. My friend's footsteps were noiseless, he seemed to glide along like one of the characters in Skelt's shilling toy theatres, still keeping in the road, but all the while abreast of me.

I was confounded, a feeling of fear came over me, I sickened at heart […] I involuntarily started off downhill as fast as my legs could take me. To my horror, he glided too, faster than ever. […] Dim pictures of horses danced past me, now up now down the hedges passed my distorted vision, railings shot up and vanished like streaks of white paint. I thought I would just turn round and scan the distance which lay atwixt me and Mr Spectre. Horror upon horrors – agony upon agony. There stood the wretch in the road, quite calm and contemplative.

My first impulse was to shout for the police, my next to seize him by the throat, and strangle him […] I saw or I fancied I saw a light, with frantic effort I bounded towards it; I seized a garden gate, it would not yield; I felt a figure glide up to me, as I stood trembling at the portal, and a warm breath whispered

in my ears, these ominous words, 'I hope you're not fatigued, sir.' It was my silent friend, my evening tormentor. I loathed him, my blood boiled, I strove to speak and failed, I strove again and prevailed, 'Do you wish to insult me?' 'No, certainly not sir,' said my tormentor, 'I only hope you are not fatigued, sir. Good night.' So saying he politely bowed and glided noiselessly away in the mist.

Whilst the anonymous letter writer does not mention a top hat, one has to wonder what well-spoken gentleman in Victorian London would not be wearing something similar on such a cold and icy night. So who – or what – is this 'Victorian' gentleman in black, who can by turns appear deceptively, even overbearingly polite, and yet also exhibits such malevolent and intimidating traits?

A Top Hat Helps Identify an 1865 Suicide Victim

At the time of writing, over 170,000 people are officially buried in Highgate Cemetery. Debate amongst paranormal enthusiasts in recent years has led to an increasing consensus that shades of the deceased, whether seemingly sentient or apparent 'stone tape' recordings of traumatic or otherwise emotional events which are being replayed from the past, tend to manifest in places that were significant to them in life, or at the moment of death. The idea of a historic graveyard and its environs being haunted simply because of the volume of bodies contained therein has become increasingly unfashionable, and there is some sense in this. But what of those who have shuffled off their mortal coil at exactly that spot?

On 1 December 1856 a cemetery labourer, named only as Collins, was piling wood in the London Cemetery Company's 'newly enclosed ground' at Highgate Cemetery. This would be what we know today as Highgate Cemetery East, the land having been purchased in 1854. The spot at which Collins stood, as he heard the chapel bells peal at 5 p.m. to signal the end of his day's work, was very near the then Cemetery superintendent's lodge. Mr Broadbent, the superintendent, seems to have made a habit of firing his shotgun at that time of day. Consequently Collins was not alarmed to hear the discharge of a firearm as the bells continued to toll. However, as darkness fell and Collins proceeded to leave the cemetery grounds, close to where the modern admission booth now stands, he stumbled upon a frightful sight.

According to *Lloyd's Weekly London News* of 7 December 1856:

the deceased, who presented the appearance of a gentlemanly-attired person, lay on the ground, with the right side of his face and head completely blown away. In his right hand the deceased grasped the stock of a pistol, and the barrel which had been blown off by the force of the explosion, lay at some distance from the body. Mr Broadbent immediately sent off to acquaint the police, who on examining the deceased's clothing minutely, found that he was dressed in dark clothing, and appeared to be a gentleman; he had a gold ring with a white stone in it on his finger, a serpent ring through which his neckerchief was passed, and a gold pin in his shirt. His linen was marked 'Henri Feuhonlet,' while under the lining of his hat were also found the initials 'H.F.' in ink. Two sealed letters were likewise found in his pocket, the one addressed to a 'Miss Partridge,' while the other, on being opened, began 'My dear father and mother;' [...] the writer spoke of great mental afflictions on account of some love affair, and ended by saying 'I can write no more'.

Enquiries by the press established that the deceased was indeed a Mr Henri Feuhonlet, of Kilmarten-terrace in nearby Holloway, the son of a gentleman and a surgeon-dentist by trade who was just 20 years old. After an inquest into his death, which returned a verdict of 'suicide whilst of unsound mind', Feuhonlet was buried in Highgate Cemetery West, not far from the spot where he passed the final and terrible moments of his short life. Could Henri Feuhonlet's tragic death account for the many sightings of a well-dressed Victorian gentleman in the Swains Lane vicinity and beyond? His doomed love life dovetails somewhat with the oral tradition which remained prevalent in The Flask some 140 years later.

Perhaps, though, if we wish to solve the mystery of just who or what this man in black is, we should be looking for more clues than a gentleman fashionably dressed in the style of the 1850s, who died alone and in great distress in Swains Lane. Victorian press reports do little in the way of furnishing readers with any further insights into Henri Feuhonlet's character and his familiarity with, or fondness for, roaming Highgate. Additionally, the top-hatted spectre has little in common with more traditional ghosts. His clothing would suggest that he has been around for at least 150 years, and yet he is not getting fainter or becoming transparent, as many other ghosts seem to. Far from being a passive, senseless shade from the past, he often interacts with those to whom he grants an audience. He speaks, very audibly. Sometimes he has a face, sometimes not. Sometimes he has such a lifelike appearance that he is mistaken for a living person, sometimes he appears to be two dimensional. And unlike ghosts who are assumed to be bound in some way to the place where they manifest, he appears to be able to move about at will. He seems a world away from the many grey ladies who are reported to self-absorbedly wander the halls of Britain's stately homes, or the battle scenes which many maintain periodically replay upon its fields.

Part of the enduring fascination and confusion which haunted Highgate holds for many lies in the homogenisation during the retelling of stories over the years of what seem to be two disparate and yet very similar entities in the vicinity. For it is certainly the case that, in addition to the man in black, less vocal apparitions of an equally commanding stature and dark appearance have also been observed in and around the cemetery, including Swains Lane, usually taking a cowled form. Whether the top-hatted spook has company, or appears in two forms, I must leave to the reader to decide.

A Cowled Figure Abroad in Swains Lane

One eyewitness account of a distressing encounter with this amorphous dark figure in Swains Lane dates back to 1965. It was recorded in 1997 by one Brian Bourne, sometimes referred to as the Revd Brian Bourne, who had by that time retired to Exeter. An ex-army officer, Brian also (perhaps somewhat incongruously) was for many years the editor of the magazine *Hedgewitch*, which catered for people and groups involved in all things esoteric, and was a long-term member of the internationally recognised Pagan order, the Fellowship of Isis.

Brian, who in 1965 was living in Islington, had been invited to a party in Highgate and had parked his car at The Flask public house in Highgate Village. At around 8 o'clock on what was a beautiful and warm summer evening, he set off for Swains Lane accompanied by his 8-year-old lurcher, enthused with thoughts of a certain girl he hoped would be at the party. Shortly after he passed the signal mast at the top of the lane and began his descent, Brian became 'uncomfortably aware of a curious silence. All the birds had suddenly stopped singing. The silence … the only way I could describe it is that it was rather like being enveloped in a large woolly blanket.' Brian continues:

> I was 10 yards from the North Gate when I happened to look across at it. What I saw was what appeared to be black treacle flowing down and running over the wall. It touched the ground and actually flowed like a big black pool of liquid into the centre of the path about 6 feet before me. There was an icy coldness which grew more intense with the passing seconds, literally an Arctic cold. The hairs on my neck, for the first time in my life, actually stood on end. With dusk falling full on the perimeter wall, the path

was in shadow, but there was a shadow discernible within that shadow. I thought, 'What am I watching? What the hell is this?' The most horrible part was – and I still have nightmares about it, still wake up in a cold sweat – it reared up. I'd estimate its height at between 7 or 8 feet. I'm 5 feet 8 inches tall and it towered over me. It was enormous. It was neither solid nor transparent. My overall impression was that it was a black figure wearing dark garments which flowed and stirred in the wind – but there was no wind. The edges of what it was wearing were moving. No face. Where eyes would have been if it were human, there were just two red pits, red glows, and I was very conscious that it was looking at me. At that point I realised that I was up against an entity that was both powerful and malignant. It was radiating evil, that's the only way I could describe it. This wasn't a ghost, this was an entity. There was nothing remotely human about it. It simply was not human. As an ex-army officer I'd come up against life-threatening situations, but faced with that thing the fear was worse than anything you could imagine.

The whole encounter according to Brian lasted just seconds, but seemed to go on for much longer. Brian's dog, who could obviously also see or sense the entity, was similarly affected and began to whine and growl in terror. The last thing Brian remembers is a feeling of paralysis, and attempting to repel the entity by visualising a banishing pentagram. This seemed to have some effect, as he recalls coming to, leaning against the wall at the top of Swains Lane having

been beaten there in his retreat by his dog. Brian's lurcher, which succumbed to a mystery illness a few days later and passed away, never fully recovered its senses, and Brian, who retreated back to The Flask for a few stiff brandies, never did get to his party.

A Young Nurse is Assaulted by the 'Ghost'

A police report, which is still on file, records another bizarre event in the lane some six years later. In 1971, a young nurse walking to the Whittington Hospital down Swains Lane one evening was allegedly thrown violently to the ground by a figure in black near the top gate of Highgate Cemetery West. Landing on her hands and knees, elbows grazed, tights torn, and staring up the lane at the dark form of her attacker, this unfortunate witness claimed that he – or it – simply dissolved in the headlights of an approaching car. Fortunately, although the motorist did not see the figure, he did notice the young woman in the middle of the road. Presuming, despite her protestations to the contrary, that she had been assaulted by a human being, he helped her to her feet and drove her to nearby Highgate Police Station, where she gave a statement. A swift manhunt was launched but no trace was ever found of who or what had attacked the young nurse. At the place where the assault occurred, the walls of Swains Lane are lined with 12- and 8ft-high stone walls.

The nurse's account does not mention whether the figure she encountered was wearing a top hat or any other discernible clothing, perhaps as a result of the

The area in Swains Lane where a young nurse was assaulted in 1971. Her assailant vanished in the headlamps of a passing car, despite the high walls and fences which border the lane. (© Dave Milner)

brevity of her dimly-lit encounter. It is also unclear whether the nurse was physically shoved or fell as a result of some aggressive supernatural force, which emanated from what she could only describe as a tall, dark figure.

The Entity Frightens a Motorist

As recently as 27 February 2005, at around 9.30 p.m., Mrs Annie Waite was driving up Swains Lane when in the near distance she saw, propped up against the cemetery wall, what at first appeared to be a large fallen tree branch. As her headlights fell fully upon the shape, she realised in some confusion that this dark 'object' was in fact a tall man dressed entirely in black. She could make out nothing of his clothing except for a hood of some kind, which seemed to envelope his head, save for his eyes. It was these more than any other aspect of his strange appearance which disturbed her, as, rather in the manner of the cats' eyes reflectors which are so common on English country roads, they seemed to be refracting the light of the headlamps. Unwilling to stop the car and concerned about reversing down a one-way street, Mrs Waite found herself within yards of the figure and overwhelmed with a feeling of nausea. Hammy as she admits it sounds, Mrs Waite recalls that whoever this weird-looking man was, he was 'full of evil'. She was relieved therefore, albeit perplexed, when the figure, seemingly disturbed by the bright lights from the car, shrank back into the cemetery wall until it had disappeared altogether. Some days later and somewhat earlier in the evening, Mrs Waite again had cause to drive up Swains Lane, but on this occasion (fortunately) there was nothing to be seen in the vicinity of her earlier sighting.

That this hooded spectre seems to emerge from and return to Highgate Cemetery West will be explored in the next chapter, when we examine some more of its apparent manifestations which have occurred within the cemetery itself.

Ghosts in the Machine?

It is not just the human senses which are assailed by some invisible force in Swains Lane. Failing mobile phone batteries and signals, and malfunctioning cameras also seem to be *de rigueur*. Fortunately, cameras do not always inexplicably refuse to perform in Swains Lane, however. Islington-raised Redmond McWilliams, founder of The Highgate Cemetery Vampire Appreciation Society has spent years studying and collating reports of strange phenomena in the Highgate area. On 9 December 2011, Redmond spent a two-hour vigil alone in Swains Lane, hoping to catch a glimpse of the ghost for himself.

Towards the end of his vigil Redmond, chilly, but in good spirits and not experiencing any negative sensations, decided to take some photographs of the West Cemetery's North Gate and its immediate environs. Although he experienced nothing of a supernatural nature at the time, when he uploaded the shots to his computer Redmond was startled to discover that four of the thirty-one image files showed unusual phenomena. The two most striking captures show a bright white mist-like

The strange, serpentine mist caught by Redmond McWilliams on camera in December 2011 and seen by three independent witnesses five months later. (© Redmond McWilliams)

form moving around inside the cemetery gates, with the same serpentine form shown in a later frame snaking down Swains Lane. This image appears to show the white mist changing direction as it bumps into an invisible form in the middle of the lane. Redmond has discounted the usual explanations for such anomalous images; he is a non-smoker, was not in the vicinity of any drains or recently parked cars and there were no obvious light sources present which could have caused the camera to produce such an effect.

Photographs which are presented as evidence of the paranormal generally get a rough ride from sceptics, debatably quite rightly. However, in May 2012, some five months after Redmond's digitally dated photographs were taken but before they had been published, a contributor to the forum 'Mumsnet' recalled the following events which suggest that whatever Redmond photographed is sometimes visible to the naked eye:

> The only time I ever witnessed anything was last Halloween [2011]. My friend and I went to Highgate village. We had a couple of beers in a pub along with a meal [...] My mate asked me to show him Highgate Cemetery. So we walked down Swains Lane for a bit and then came back up. On approaching the North Gate I saw what appeared to be 'white wisps' being pulled through the railings of the North Gate. I shouted 'Look' then ran to the gate. A man walking his dog came down the hill. When he got level with the gate the dog went berserk and starting straining on his lead so much the man had to go back up the hill.

The Ghost of a Body Snatcher

Before we leave Swains Lane, we should take note of a sighting which differs significantly from those so far discussed. It occurred in June 2012, to members of North London Paranormal Investigations (NLPI), a group which uses a combination of modern technology and mediumistic intuition to research haunted sites along the Northern Heights of London, and this author interviewed the witnesses a few days later. That evening, co-founders Mickey and Louise Gocool were showing a new member of their team around some 'haunted' locales on their patch. Gemma Pugh, an Essex-based medium, was standing in the vicinity of Highgate Cemetery's main gates at around 10.30 p.m. with Mickey, when both claim to have seen the fleeting apparition of a man in early 1800s attire. Although he was not wearing a top hat, he was relatively smartly dressed, and seemed to want to give the impression of being from 'good stock'. Louise, unfortunately, was further up the lane at the time and did not see this 'gentleman' – who professed in a clairvoyant series of impressions received by Gemma to have been an undertaker in life.

The spirit which Gemma claims to have made contact with did not seem to unnerve the team. Moreover, they felt that he was a remorseful soul, a self-proclaimed 'lawyer' from central London who had taken over the family undertaking business reluctantly and had made regrettable decisions when its fortunes declined. Specifically, according to Gemma's interpretation, the figure claimed to have illegally sold bodies, and later 'burked' four people – that is, dispatched them for their bodies in the style of notorious 1820s murderers Burke and Hare. The illicit trade in human corpses, stolen from their graves by night for sale to surgeons at London's medical schools, flourished in Britain throughout the eighteenth and early nineteenth centuries. At this time the only cadavers legally obtainable for dissection were those of certain convicted criminals. The fact that the fresher the corpse was, the more it was worth, made the practice of 'burking' more lucrative than the traditional means employed by body snatchers (or resurrection men, as they were known).

As an interesting aside, throughout the first half of the twentieth century it was 'established knowledge' amongst pupils of Tollington Park School in nearby Tufnell Park (where Johnny Rotten of punk band the Sex Pistols *sometimes* turned up to school) that the man who haunted Swains Lane was guarding the body of his son. That the children believed a priori that a man of some supernatural persuasion was haunting the lane over fifteen years before any such story made it into the popular press is interesting in itself. Urban legend from that period dictates that this was the ghost of a tragic father who lost his son to tuberculosis at a young age and, fearing the body snatchers who were then operating around North London, buried him illicitly in an unmarked grave in Highgate Cemetery. Still not content that his child's mortal remains would rest in peace, he patrolled the gravesite nightly, even after death. Romantic as it is, this schoolboys' tale lacks historical accuracy, as the cemetery's construction postdates the époque of the resurrection men. More likely origins are the real-life working-class stories which

tell of deceased infants from poorer families being placed 'hush hush' in the coffins of those who could afford them. For a tip of two shillings and sixpence to Highgate Cemetery's chapel staff, this was common practice until at least 1943.

But what of the 'gentleman' who so earnestly accosted NLPI with his tale of woe and appeals for forgiveness? Perhaps, despite their well-meaning intentions, the last laugh was on them. For it is undoubtedly true that a compulsive liar, John Bishop, of West Hill which partly encircles Highgate Cemetery West, was hanged in 1831 for his role in a body-snatching enterprise which devolved into 'burking'. Suspicion was attracted by a physician at King's College, London, who found the body of a teenaged boy proffered to him for sale by Bishop to be 'suspiciously fresh'. Far from inheriting a family undertaking business (a description which could hardly be applied to the London Cemetery Company), Bishop was forced to take over his father's Highgate-based carting firm when Bishop Snr passed away suddenly after losing both legs in an accident on Archway Road. Not destined for a respectable career, and with the business already in competition with larger carting firms, Bishop adopted the ruse of delivering goods up and down West Hill to transport stolen corpses from neighbouring churchyards to the city. He also enjoyed a sideline as a professional 'grass' and false alibi – meaning that he did indeed have many occasions to visit legal premises in the heart of London.

Contemporary portraits of Bishop in early 1800s dress, with his lack of hat, aquiline nose, high cheekbones and generally well-bred features, do suggest a physical resemblance to the apparition described by Mickey and Gemma. The Anatomy Act, which brought an end to the revolting trade of body snatching, was passed in 1832, as a direct result of Bishop and his accomplices' convictions, and some seven years before Highgate Cemetery was opened to the public. Whether Bishop, who was himself dissected for the purposes of science, really holds any regrets or still haunts his old stomping grounds will remain forever a matter of conjecture, as does the capacity of professional liars to continue to obfuscate the truth 'in spirit'. The 'spirit' encountered in June 2012 allegedly remarked that he was amused by the popular misconception that he was a 'vampire'. Police informant becomes lawyer, resurrection man becomes undertaker. Perhaps, if he was indeed the shade of Bishop, he also gained amusement from spinning this inverted version of his life to a breathlessly fascinated audience.

Tracing rumours to their source can sometimes assist with the identification of possible 'ghosts' – or at least their origins. Asked to name a burial ground near Highgate, nine out of ten people would choose Highgate Cemetery. Purists, however, would point out the existence of the small churchyard attached to the former chapel of ease opposite The Gatehouse. Like the graveyards in Holloway, this was targeted by resurrection men. In 1817, in the transcript of an unrelated court case, we find two nightwatchmen routinely keeping a vigil by the railings which surround the chapel. One body snatcher, writing under the pseudonym 'Jack Ketch' with reference to his later vocation as an executioner, recalled in an autobiographical sketch published in *The Metropolitan* magazine in 1835:

> I remained upwards of three years a resurrectionist […] The surgeon whom I especially served was a remarkable man for selecting his own subjects, and few of his friends on whom he had placed his eye while living, escaped his knife when dead. I was sent for one day, and told that a relation of his, recently dead, who was buried in Highgate churchyard, must be had. Unwilling to disoblige or lose a good customer, we went down two successive nights, but failed, which put our employer in a towering passion. To appease him I was determined to make another attempt, and try what a bribe would do with the watchman: I however had no sooner made an offer in a public-house to which I had invited him before the watch was set, than he seized me, and calling for assistance, took me before a magistrate.

Whether or not Bishop was bold enough to obtain his 'merchandise' from quite so close to home, we will never know. We do know that it is very unlikely that the cemetery was targeted by body snatchers in the nineteenth century, but that the churchyard 100 yards or so to the north *was* thus afflicted. It is certainly possible that some early tales about fear of body snatching, surviving by word of mouth, have conflated the two historic sites and in the spirit of good storytelling at some stage acquired a paranormal element. This could just feasibly account for the Tollington Park pupils' notions about the origins of the ghost of nearby Highgate Cemetery.

All of this interesting speculation aside, there may be a much more direct explanation for the rumour. Acclaimed war photographer Don McCullin and his younger brother Michael were pupils at the school, and in 1962 Don composed a very bizarre character portrait of an acquaintance of theirs who lived in Mercers Road, Upper Holloway. The photograph, titled variously 'The Headhunter of Highgate' or 'Collector of Death', depicts a man perhaps in his late twenties, holding a bamboo cane in each hand surmounted by a human skull. This man, who strongly resembles a young Charlie Manson, had been known to the McCullins since their schooldays. In the early years of their friendship he confessed fairly openly to the boys not only that he was 'heavily into black magic', but that with a group of similarly inclined deviants he regularly obtained skulls and even whole skeletons in their coffins from Highgate and Kensal Green Cemeteries. According to an interview given in 1980, McCullin and his brother were fascinated by the bones, human hair, bottles of formaldehyde and coffin-opening toolkits which littered the rank-smelling basement flat. If tales of this modern-day body snatcher influenced generations of schoolchildren and cemented an urban myth, we can at least discount one of the many back stories afforded to the spectre of Swains Lane. And so the search for his true origins goes on ...

2

HIGHGATE CEMETERY WEST[1]

Highgate Cemetery West is without doubt one of the most famous cemeteries in the world. Like Paris's Père Lachaise, it remains at the top of many people's wish lists of places to visit at least once in their lifetime. While the cemetery's haunted reputation has also acquired global fame, it would be unfair to suggest that this is the primary reason why this ivy-encumbered Victorian necropolis, with its crumbling edifices, finds itself on the international tourist map. This it owes chiefly to the gothic splendour of its design, the hundreds of ornate memorials which have been lavished upon it over the years, and the constant battle which is visibly being fought between man's constructs and the will of nature. Two terms coined by the Friends of Highgate Cemetery (FOHC) capture the essence of this extraordinary landscape perfectly, for it surely is a 'Victorian Valhalla', suspended in a perpetual state of 'managed neglect'.

Still a working cemetery, but for some decades now offering guided tours, Highgate Cemetery is today managed by a dedicated team of staff and volunteers.

Formed in 1975 in response to the cemetery's closure by the United Cemetery Company for financial reasons, the FOHC has fought a long battle to preserve for the nation this beautiful space which was at one point threatened by the bulldozer.

Highgate Cemetery West, which covers approximately 17 acres and is dedicated to St James, was originally devised between 1836 and 1839 by architect and inventor Stephen Geary. Ironically, Geary's own grave remained lost amidst the cemetery's sprawling mass of vines and fallen branches until the late 1970s. In the year that Geary began drafting his plans, an Act of Parliament had been

The approach to the main gates of Highgate Cemetery West. (© Lorcan Maguire)

passed, allowing his fledgling London Cemetery Company (which survived until 1960) to establish six private cemeteries around the capital.

The ever-increasing population of mid-nineteenth-century London had by this time led to an extreme shortage of burial plots, with many graves being reused and any available patches of land being appropriated for use as impromptu and makeshift graveyards. Highgate was the third private cemetery to be opened in an attempt to tackle this issue, initially providing space for 30,000 graves. It takes its place amongst the group of architectural extravaganzas built between 1832 and 1841 known today as 'The Magnificent Seven', the others being Kensal Green, West Norwood, Abney Park, Nunhead, Brompton and Tower Hamlets.

The Victorian cult of death ensured that these cemeteries were nothing like the rustic parish churchyards which had for centuries ensconced the mortal remains of their architects' ancestors. Drawing upon Egyptian and classical influences, these cities of the dead reflected the importance placed by Victorians upon enshrining the memories of the departed through increasingly elaborate means. Imposing ground-level mausoleums, set amongst dramatically landscaped promenades such as Highgate's famous Egyptian Avenue, not only allowed mourners to demonstrate just how much they were prepared to spend upon their dead; they also made paying one's respects a social event. Some of these moneyed mourners' contemporaries found this practice rather distasteful, as we learn from George Collison's 1840 work *Cemetery Interment*:

One is so much accustomed to associate ideas of pleasure and holiday making with Highgate and its beautiful vicinity, that a cemetery seems almost the last place we should think of meeting with there; and so little is the former feeling subdued by the general associations of the place, that the author has seen parties of pleasure partaking of their slight refreshments, in rural language called pic-nic, within the consecrated area.

Indeed in the early days of Highgate Cemetery's initial popularity, it was quite the fashion for its visitors to take tea on the roof of the Terrace Catacombs, enjoying the unrivalled views over London which were later blighted by the erection of the enormous Julius Beer Mausoleum.

Essentially an 80ft-long stone passageway, each wall lined with shelves upon which coffin after coffin lies neatly stacked, the interior of the Terrace Catacombs has a somewhat claustrophobic atmosphere. Illuminated only by natural light, which filters through thick opaque glass set into small apertures in the flat roof, it could not contrast more strongly with the jolly parties which were once held within feet of its sleeping incumbents.

While many of London's elite fell over themselves to purchase the grandest vaults available in the coveted Circle of Lebanon, no doubt visualising their own funeral processions solemnly advancing down the otherworldly Egyptian Avenue, not all commentators were impressed by this pre-mortem snobbery. A humorous review published in 1840 of a handbill, produced by the London Cemetery Company and advertising an astonishing range of added-on charges for all things funereal, warns the public to:

beware of being 'emboweled' in the 'mother earth' of Highgate Cemetery 'before three o'clock P.M.,' or 'after sunset;' it will cost you, else, an additional seven shillings and sixpence. Funeral officials are asleep, or busy, betimes in the morning, and after sundown they catch cold. If there be a keen north-easter astir, you may have the 'use of a large Weather-Screen' for the small charge of half a sovereign and one sixpence. If you […] are desirous of revelling in the 'Privilege of placing a Head and Foot Stone to a Grave' (our quotations are exact!) you must see after the vampire 'powers that be', and with them mutually sign, seal, and deliver, 'a Special Agreement'.

Before the cemetery's construction the land was privately occupied. Built by Sir William Ashurst (1647–1720), at various times Director of the Bank of England and Mayor of London, Ashurst House was an imposing, southerly facing mansion of square dimensions. Once occupying the land upon which St Michael's church was constructed in 1831 under the direction of Lewis Vulliamy, it enjoyed beautifully landscaped grounds which extended south down Highgate's West Hill. The grand topography of these pleasure gardens is clearly visible in two surviving prints from 1688 and 1710, and it is immediately apparent from these bird's-eye views that many of their paths and features were incorporated into the present-day cemetery. A survivor of these is the distinctive Cedar of Lebanon, the large and exotic tree, surmounting the sunken circle of tombs near the top of the cemetery from which the labyrinthine Circle of Lebanon takes its name.

Perplexingly, for a luxurious villa in such a pleasantly situated location, no tenants seem to have resided for very long at Ashurst House. The estate passed through the ownership of Sir William's son and grandson before it was sold out of the family. It was then leased to a series of tenants, and for a brief period was the home of a school, but by this time its grounds had been left in a ruinous condition and were entirely neglected. Sheep and cattle

The sunken Circle of Lebanon in Highgate Cemetery. (© Della Farrant)

grazed freely upon what had once been manicured lawns and elaborate topiary.

Abandoned and in a dangerous state of repair, Ashurst House was finally demolished in 1830. As so many listed buildings survive in Highgate Village today, treasured and restored to their former glory, the mansion's fate is relatively unusual. Indeed, we learn from C.V. Thompson (*The Cholmeley Grammar School at Highgate*, 1923) that 'the ground was purchased advantageously as the house, having a reputation for being haunted, had stood empty for many years'. Remnants of the house can still be found in various parts of Highgate Village. These, coupled with the many nods which Highgate Cemetery West's undulations give to its predecessor, enhance the sense that in Highgate nothing is really lost forever. An 1813 town house in the High Street has for its portico the original of the old mansion, replete with a moulded architrave bearing the Ashurst arms, evidently salvaged wholesale from the wreckage. In nearby Broadbent Close, named for the owner of the saw-pits which once existed here and produced thousands of coffins for Geary's cemeteries, a mysterious folly still stands which is thought to have been constructed from the old house's supporting walls. Even the once lavishly stocked wine cellars today form part of the crypt of St Michael's church, enshrining the tomb of the poet Samuel Taylor Coleridge.

The dramatic decline in the maintenance of the once beautiful gardens of Ashurst House is mirrored in the deplorable condition of Highgate Cemetery by the late 1960s. Over the previous four decades, changes in funerary customs, the increasing popularity of cremations, and the impact of the two world wars had led to an escalating neglect of its tombs and chapels. Some burials were still taking place, and the role of gravedigger continues in the same family line to this day. Tragically, however, many of the men who made up the large team of gardeners were called up to fight, never to return, and with the cemetery's flora and fauna left unchecked, nature rapidly began to take the upper hand. It is against this backdrop of gothic corrosion that many stories of something uncanny at work in the cemetery begin to emerge fully.

A Hooded Figure Peering over the Wall

Paul Quinn contacted this author some years back with some fascinating stories of the supernatural told to him by his father Michael, who grew up in Highgate. Mr Quinn Snr remembers scrumping for apples in the grounds of Parkhurst House, which was demolished to make way for the Hillcrest Estate in the 1940s (Hillcrest's own haunted reputation is discussed in Chapter 5). Mr Quinn's paranormal experiences, however, largely took place some small distance south, at Highgate Cemetery West.

Between 1960 and 1968 Mr Quinn was employed by Bates Nurseries, who leased land at the 2-acre site at the back of Highgate High Street which continued to be used for the cultivation of plants, fruit and vegetables until 2013. The nursery had an amicable relationship with the superintendent of Highgate Cemetery, supplying flowers for graves maintained 'in perpetuity' at a reduced rate, in return for the use of felled wood, compost and other arboricultural waste. Paul recalls:

> I remember Dad telling me that they used to have permission from the people who ran the cemetery to collect bean sticks for growing the beans up in the nursery. One winter evening in 1962 my father and his workmate were collecting the wood. It was a cold evening anyway but both of them felt chilled to the bone. Opposite them was a 6-foot wall, and they froze on the spot as both saw a hooded figure rising above this wall. My father described it as something with a conical head, rather like a monk's hood.

Another evening around 1968, Mr Quinn was returning to the nursery via Swains Lane when he recalls glimpsing through the cemetery's North Gate 'the figure of a darkly dressed man who looked like he was wearing a top hat', standing or hovering in a patch of mist some 15 feet down the path. As Mr Quinn rapidly crossed the narrow lane and grabbed the locked gates for a better look at the figure, it slowly dissolved into the mist. Mr Quinn states that there was no noise of someone running away.

Spirit Voices Recorded on Tape

In 1965, Holloway-based Joe Meek (who found fame as the world's first independent record producer) approached David Farrant, whose name is now synonymous with what the press have since 1970 referred to as the 'Highgate Vampire',

The North Gate at Highgate Cemetery. Perhaps one of the most haunted locations in Highgate, it is here that many people claim to have seen a tall, dark figure hovering inside on the path, or standing beside it in Swains Lane. (© Dave Milner)

with some tape recordings he had made during what had become regular nocturnal visits to Highgate Cemetery West. Meek believed that these tapes had captured the voices of spirits active in the cemetery, and indeed the tapes do seem to contain the sound of a female voice, speaking in distant and distorted sentences. Subsequently, Farrant and Meek visited the cemetery together one afternoon, where Meek indicated that he had made the recordings on a path just above the Circle of Lebanon. It was around this time that Meek's obsession with the supernatural, and specifically the possibility of communicating with the departed, became dangerously out of control. What may have been a natural psychic ability, coupled with an undiagnosed mental illness, caused Meek to experience intense bouts of paranoia and in February 1967 he fatally shot his landlady, before turning his single-barrelled shotgun on himself.

After travelling around Europe throughout 1966, Farrant returned to Highgate in January 1967 to find the village buzzing with gossip about an extreme encounter with a ghost by the landlord of The Gatehouse public house. His interest piqued, later that year Farrant founded the organisation now known as the British Psychic and Occult Society (BPOS). The society's original membership was comprised of a cross-fertilisation of members of the Wiccan coven which Farrant then attended and local people with an active interest in ghosts and other unexplained occurrences, but quickly expanded to encompass a national remit. While many commentators have published anecdotal references to some of the hauntings discussed in this book, very few have conducted field research and none has compiled original witness interviews on the scale of the BPOS. It is this organisation's meticulous records which provide us with many invaluable contemporary reports.

A 1969 Sighting near the Circle of Lebanon

By the summer of 1969 'Farrant' had become a byword in Highgate for all things spooky, and word of mouth ensured that any publicly acknowledged 'hauntings' in the area inevitably came to his attention. One August evening in 1969, Di Compton, the mother of the landlord of The Prince of Wales public house, excitedly conveyed a personal conversation she had had with a lunchtime regular earlier that day. With Di as a go-between, a meeting was swiftly arranged between this gentleman, a resident of North Hill, and David Farrant at The Red Lion and Sun. During this rather hushed rendezvous, Farrant learned that the man, who settled upon the pseudonym 'Thornton' for the benefit of his career as a respected chartered accountant, had had a very strange experience in Highgate Cemetery West.

Thornton, a smartly dressed man in his late thirties, relayed that he made a weekday routine of driving up to Highgate during his lunch break for a cooked meal. A few weeks previously, with an unusually empty diary, Thornton decided to work off his lunch with a stroll around Highgate Cemetery. A keen amateur photographer, he spent over two hours carefully composing shots of stone angels and obscure monoliths, until the distant ringing of a bell signalled that the cemetery gates would soon be locked.

Thornton relayed to David Farrant with some embarrassment what happened next, and Farrant in turn published the account in his 1991 book *Beyond the Highgate Vampire*:

> Not being a superstitious person or even believing in ghosts, [Thornton] walked calmly around looking for the gate when he suddenly became aware of the presence of something behind him. Swinging around, less than six feet away, he saw a tall dark spectre hovering just above the ground. He found himself transfixed to the spot, completely unable to move; drained of energy by some powerful 'hypnotic force' that in a matter of seconds rendered him unconscious to any sense of time or being able to recognise his surroundings. So great was the intensity of this force, that he remained like this for several minutes (or what seemed like several minutes) before the spectre abruptly vanished and he slowly regained his normal faculties.

It is interesting to ponder whether the bells which heralded Thornton's sighting are in any way connected with Henri Feuhonlet's 1856 suicide, which took place seconds after the bell was rung to signal the cemetery's closure for the day.

The Ghost Confronts Some More of its Neighbours

A month later another friend in the village helped arrange a meeting between Farrant and an elderly female friend who had told her of a terrifying experience in Swains Lane a few days previously. Approaching 70 years of age but still very sprightly, this lady, who lived in a first-floor apartment on the Holly Lodge Estate, twice a day walked her small dog up and down Swains Lane. Until one evening in September 1969 she had experienced nothing untoward during these preambles. Over a pot of tea served with her best china set, she volunteered to Farrant that one evening after sundown she was walking her dog past the cemetery's main gates when something inside the West Cemetery caught the animal's attention. Alarmed by the dog's sudden barking and growling, the lady followed its line of vision and was startled to see a 'tall, dark man' hovering just above the ground inside the gates. As he floated towards her, the witness recalled that the strange man vanished before her eyes as swiftly as he had appeared.

A similar account was relayed to one Terry Little and surfaced some forty or so years later in a letter to the *Fortean Times* (FT296, January 2013). Little's letter concerned a sighting by Dr Charlotte Bach, who had moved into Langbourne Mansions on the Holly Lodge Estate in 1961. A close friend of well-respected occult author and sociologist Colin Wilson, in the mid to late 1960s Bach told Little of a 'frightening encounter [...] with a huge, towering dark presence near the cemetery'. Little recalls that 'she was visibly disturbed on recounting the event, raising her hands high to emphasise the height of the ghoulish figure'. Upon her death at Highgate in 1981 it was discovered that Dr Bach had been born a man, despite living the majority of her life in the public eye as a woman. Little describes Bach as being about 6 feet tall, and 'not the sort of person easily intimidated'.

A Fiend with Red Glowing Eyes?

Over the last forty years, generic descriptions of the Highgate entity invariably attribute to it the red glowing eyes of all one's 'better monsters'. With the exception of Brian Bourne, no witnesses have actually described its eyes in such a way, and even Brian's account does not suggest oversized spheres of flame. If anything, most witnesses concur that the entity's eyes seem to glint, and reflect light, giving them a mesmerising and transfixing effect. This was the case when David Farrant encountered it for himself in 1969.

Unaware of the experiences of Dr Bach, Brian Bourne and Michael Quinn, Farrant decided to visit the cemetery himself, in his words 'attempting to find some logical explanation' for what Thornton and the elderly lady had described to him. On Sunday, 21 December 1969 he left his Highgate flat at around eleven in the evening, and made the ten-minute walk to Swains Lane. His intention, as he somewhat sheepishly admits today, was to scale the main gates and head to the flat area of land near the Circle of Lebanon where Thornton's sighting had occurred. Farrant was not optimistic about his chances of encountering the spectre, so was surprised when, upon reaching the cemetery boundary at the top of the lane, he received the sudden impression that he was no longer alone.

A young David Farrant, recounting his disturbing 1969 sighting of a malevolent, tall dark figure in Swains Lane for Thames Television, 1970. (© David Farrant)

Glancing towards the North Gate, Farrant thought he discerned a movement inside. That night the moon was nearly full, but despite this the path, framed by inky black trees on both sides, was visible only for a distance of around 10 yards. As Farrant peered through the bars, scrutinising the interplay of shadows, branches and tombstones, he became aware of a humanoid shape, around 7 feet in height, which was seemingly materialising in the centre of the path. Transfixed, Farrant watched as it moved closer, stopping some 3 yards in front of him. By now afforded a much clearer view of the figure, Farrant struggled to reconcile logical thought with what hovered before him. Any suspicion that it could be of human origin was soon annulled when the surrounding area turned icy cold. At this moment Farrant describes becoming aware of two faint points of light suspended in the region of what now appeared to be a face with no other discernible features. As Farrant recalls, 'the whole situation seemed unreal – like some unwanted dream – but with determined effort I tore my gaze away, realising that the entity was malevolent and that I had come under psychic attack'.

Farrant claims to have recited a Qabalistic incantation, an occultic method by which malignant earthly influences can be negated, by the intercession of (in this case) the sphere of Tiphareth. This energetic plane is described as radiating beauty and light, concepts which seemed to disturb the entity. Like Brian Bourne's 1965 use of such methods, the visualisation seems to have been successful, as the entity instantly retreated and the temperature returned to normal, as swiftly as the picture on a television set which has just been switched off.

An Early Investigation into the Phenomena

What were now three confirmed sightings of what seemed to be the same entity were debated by members of Farrant's society, and it was agreed that the unusual degree of malice which it exhibited justified an organised inquiry. This involved members going to the cemetery during the daytime in an effort to garner other witness accounts, as well as nocturnal vigils conducted in pairs in an attempt to obtain photographic evidence of the entity. This material 'proof' was not forthcoming, but during these many cold and lonely hours one pair of volunteers did have significant sightings, the first in late December 1969 and the second in January 1970. Two male members, keeping watch at what had become referred to as the 'Thornton spot', were alarmed by a movement in their peripheral vision, and upon turning around they simultaneously saw a figure identical in appearance to that described by Thornton. Despite their best endeavours, the speed of this encounter rendered taking a photograph impossible. A week later the same members again reported seeing a darkly clad figure whilst passing the North Gate, again hovering some distance away on the path which leads towards the Terrace Catacombs. As usual, the figure quickly disappeared.

Farrant was by this time receiving regular telephone calls from various *Ham & High* reporters at the behest of the newspaper's then editor Gerald Isaaman, asking for his opinion about any newsworthy items they came across of a paranormal or occult nature, and it was suggested by one reporter that he write a letter appealing for more witnesses.

David Farrant surveying a vandalised coffin in the Terrace Catacombs, 1970. (© David Farrant)

On 6 February 1970, the *Ham & High* published his letter. Aware that entering the cemetery at night was technically illegal, Farrant carefully played down his ongoing investigation into the apparition, and to allay public concern also avoided mentioning its apparently negative nature. The letter relayed his own sighting of a 'ghost-like figure inside the gates at the top of Swains Lane' in December 1969, and out of respect for his colleagues' privacy also attributed to himself the two later sightings by members of his society. Farrant's letter prompted four initial reader responses which were published the following week with the strapline 'The ghost of N6'. These were accompanied by an invitation from the newspaper for other readers to tell their ghostly stories, and a warning that it would 'check the authenticity of all letters received' lest anyone tried to 'spoof them with spooks'. As Isaaman remembered in an interview with the *Camden New Journal* in 2009, 'in they poured', and over the next six weeks a further eighteen 'ghost' letters were published.

The range of supernatural encounters reported by readers was vast, with some recurring themes. Many locals made reference to ghostly figures appearing at night in Swains Lane and within the cemetery itself, including a 'most unusual form' which 'just seemed to glide across the path'; 'a pale figure [which] has been appearing for several years'; a soundless '"form" moving behind some gravestones'; a 'figure' in Swains Lane which appeared from nowhere only to run towards the witness and then vanish; and a 'terrible apparition' seen gloating through the bars of the main cemetery gate.

The week after Mr Docherty's letter to the *Ham & High* regarding the top-hatted ghost was published (see Chapter 1), Miss C. Stringer of 78 Woodland Gardens, N10 also wrote to the newspaper. 'The ghost startled a friend and myself when we were returning home from night duty,' she recalled. 'Being nurses we are able to deal with most situations, but the ghost, which seemed to be walking towards us from inside the gates, sent us running up Swains Lane as fast as we could.'

A Modern Intrusion

That the 'ghost of N6' had become a fashionable topic of conversation in Highgate Village provides only a partial explanation for the epidemic of paranormal encounters recorded from the late 1960s through to the early 1970s. Accusations of hoaxing, or at best the influence of auto-suggestion upon 'witnesses', are frequently offered by cynics as a simple solution to this riddle. So many unconnected witnesses relaying similar experiences within such a close time span, suggests, however, that there could be some other nexus. One trend observed by notable parapsychologists over the years, including members of the London-based Society for Psychical Research's various committees, is the apparent role which structural changes to old buildings and landscapes can play in triggering psychical phenomena. The reasons for this are unclear, but it may be significant that in 1967 the acclaimed architect John Winter began the construction of what is known as the Cor-Ten House at 81 Swains Lane. This steel and glass three-storey building stands at an impressive 2,220 square feet, and was built on land adjacent to the 1870s home of the cemetery superintendent and the disused stonemason's yard. Taking nearly three years to complete, Winter's project is largely hidden from sight by the cemetery wall, with its west side facing directly on to the cemetery itself. The proximity of the house to the main cemetery gates where so much activity has been reported is striking. Could the sinking of deep foundations within the cemetery, and the magnitude of the building work involved in the development of the Cor-Ten house, have reawakened something much older?

Interestingly, although the Cor-Ten house was home to Winter and his family for many years, none of the three Winter children who grew up in the house professes to remember anything untoward about their childhood. Winter's wife Val even ran a playgroup for local toddlers in one of the rooms which can boast Highgate Cemetery as its fenceless back garden. If the house's construction is in any way connected with the spate of encounters with a tall, dark figure around the lane, then perhaps it enjoys the calm described by meteorologists as 'the eye of the storm'.

In 1980, Winter began project managing the erection of another modernist house, slightly further up Swains Lane and just north of the main gates. The site chosen was of some historical significance, having previously been the home of a prominent and philanthropic doctor from the plague era known as Elisha Coysh, who occupied a cottage on the site from 1657. In later years, houses on and around what had been Coysh's plot became utilised as what can only be described as 'doss houses', in which originated the only recorded outbreaks of cholera in what was an otherwise sanitary district. The board of the London Cemetery Company must have breathed a literal sigh of relief when in the 1880s they finally acquired the vacant possession of these disease-ridden and tumbledown cottages with their stinking cowsheds and overflowing privies, which had been the scene of so many agonising deaths.

This modern house was also demolished, in 2005, after the property was observed to be leaning upon the adjacent cemetery walls, and a new four-storey building was erected. The theory that significant structural changes to buildings can influence supernatural manifestations may also go some way towards explaining Martin Trent and Annie Waite's 2005 encounters with figures of alleged supernatural origin in Swains Lane, a hypothesis which has been posited by David Farrant in recent years.

Black Magic among the Monuments

By the 1960s Highgate Cemetery had become attractive to a variety of magical orders, which used its open spaces and vaults at night for their rituals. In an interview with this author, Melusine Draco, author of *Traditional Witchcraft and the Pagan Revival* (2013), remembered the allure which Highgate Cemetery held for her own group:

> The atmosphere at Highgate Cemetery in the early 1970s was deliciously 'dark' – not in an evil or sinister sense but as a place where Otherworld was only a step away. I have always been drawn to those 'dark' energies which are best described as chthonic – of the deep earth, or ancient ancestral energies. In those days there were lots of other groups and/or individuals using the Cemetery, but Craft has its own unwritten rule that out of respect you don't work on someone else's patch. We had our 'secret corners' and they had theirs; and never the twain did meet!

Some white magicians, however, became concerned about the activities of a group of necromancers, the remains of whose rituals had been found in the Cory-Wright mausoleum. Specifically, they suspected that these ceremonial magicians had evoked extremely negative forces, and that these were responsible for the aggressive manifestations of a tall, dark figure to so many civilians. As Melusine points out:

> A lot depends on the intended outcome of the working as to whether a burial ground is the right place to hold the ritual. After all, Highgate Cemetery for all its majesty and beauty is contrived woodland that only happened as a result of neglect and decay. Surely no one would cast a spell on a burial site without expecting some kind of negative outcome, and there was often a great feeling of sadness about the place.

On the night of the Summer Solstice in 1971 seven members of the British Psychic and Occult Society conducted a carefully planned ritual near the Circle of Lebanon, in an attempt to exorcise the force which had 'invaded' the cemetery and environs. Although they were unable to achieve this, shortly after midnight the invocations of a psychic medium allegedly caused the entity to manifest briefly. As the candles around the protective circle flickered out, a mist descended. Through this was discernible a writhing black shadow, which was forming in the small triangle intended to contain it. As it increased in height, two glinting points of light became visible, which appeared to represent its eyes. It seems that even magical orders

Remains of necromantic rituals discovered in the Cory-Wright family vault at Highgate Cemetery. (© David Farrant)

comply with Health and Safety guidelines, for as one girl fainted and the medium herself became overwhelmed, it was decided that the entity should be promptly banished, unfortunately before it could be interrogated.

Enter the Vampire

An earlier attempt to conduct a similar séance had been disrupted in August 1970, and resulted in David Farrant's arrest for 'vampire hunting'. Among Farrant's possessions seized that night were the pre-requisite candles, incense and charcoal and, maybe optimistically, a camera. He was also carrying some chalk, and a carved piece of wood with a length of white satin cord attached, with which the group intended to mark out their protective circle. Perhaps in a misguided attempt to make clear that there were legal consequences for would-be vampire hunters, when Farrant's case was heard the police ensured that the wooden stake was presented bereft of its white cord. It now resembled, to all intents and purposes, a stake straight out of a Hollywood vampire movie.

The police's mindset in this regard may seem ludicrous and shocking to a modern reader, but it must be understood that in February and March that year, shortly after the *Ham & High* published its readers' 'ghost' letters, it had run a series of sensationalist headlines such as 'Does a Wampyr Walk in Highgate?' and 'Why do the Foxes Die?' 'What nonsense it all was. It was a real hoot, and we played the story for laughs,' Gerald Isaaman, the then editor, recalled thirty-eight years later. At a time when the Hammer House of

Horror was regularly filming on location in the overgrown cemetery, the 'ghost' was quickly hijacked by the national media, but by now it had morphed into a blood-sucking vampire. Following a Thames TV broadcast in which extremely irresponsible comments were made, hundreds of people descended upon the cemetery on the night of Friday, 13 March 1970, causing incredible damage.

The judge dismissed the police's case against Farrant, and subsequent coverage of the bizarre charge of vampire hunting in local and national newspapers and on television merely inspired even more vandals, intent upon finding the 'vampire'. A present-day tour guide remembers, in his youth, mistaking Christopher Lee, who was filming in Highgate and still in costume, for a real-life vampire. Despite no bodies drained of blood ever being discovered, and no police inquiry, vampire mania seized the public imagination. The residents of Highgate, who had been quite content with their local ghost, were far less enthused. Today, as then, the subject of the 'Highgate vampire' is met with disdain at the luncheon clubs of the elite, in the local pubs, and especially by the Friends of Highgate Cemetery. These new tales of a vampire brought nothing but trouble to Highgate; children were now afraid to sleep at night, and drunken youths from out of town were jumping over the cemetery gates,

SATAN RIDDLE OF OPEN TOMB

Two youths scale the cemetery gates during the hunt for the vampire.

Crowds of young people gather outside Highgate Cemetery's North Gate during the great 'vampire hunt' of Friday, 13 March 1970. (© London Evening News)

staking corpses, then bragging in the local bars about the skulls and bones which they had 'liberated' from the Victorian coffins. Johnny Rotten recalls in his 1993 autobiography *No Irish, No Blacks, No Dogs*: 'So many people were doing it … loonies mostly, running around with wooden stakes, crucifixes and cloves of garlic … it was almost like a social club down there.'

In 1975 the cemetery was closed to the public, and the vandalism eventually died down. It seems that the sole legacy left by this vampire in its fictitious wake was the damage which, even today, dedicated volunteers are still making good. Perhaps it is therefore understandable that even discussing the imaginary vampire is frowned upon by exasperated tour guides, who with their wealth of knowledge about real notables interred in the cemetery are frequently asked to point out where 'the king vampire of the undead' sleeps. As one long-standing volunteer quipped, with some gravitas, in 2013: 'To paraphrase from *The Lost Boys*: one thing about volunteering at Highgate I never could stomach … all the damn vampires.' But fortunately for paranormal enthusiasts, the ghost or ghosts which innocently started it all, seem to live on.

A Ghostly Figure on Film?

The slow termination of this era of chaos from 1975 onwards also seems to have had an effect upon the ghost. As the cemetery's new management team settled down, so it seems did the spectre, with the 1980s representing a notable lull in reports of its manifestations. But true to its apparently cyclical and certainly secretive nature, it had not vanished for good.

Many visitors to Highgate Cemetery who are aware of its haunted reputation vainly hope that they will be 'lucky' enough to encounter one of its ghosts for themselves. Sightings from within the cemetery, however, do seem to be rare, as are daylight confrontations with the entity in general. Unsurprisingly, with this in mind, the thousands of photographs taken by visitors and uploaded to the internet have yet to reveal an inadvertently captured apparition. The fact that so many photographs exist of the cemetery contrasts sharply with the previously discussed technical anomalies reported in Swains Lane. One account of mechanical malfunction certainly stands out, however.

A contributor now living in Frome, Somerset, who wishes to be referred to only as Martin, contacted this author in 2014 with the most extreme case of malfunctioning electronic equipment in the cemetery which has emerged to date. In November 1989, whilst a student at Camberwell Art College, Martin and twelve members of his photography class, along with their tutor, took part in a 'visual research' field trip to Highgate Cemetery. Martin recalls that although their outing commenced on:

[a] glorious crisp morning with bright sunshine, once we entered the cemetery, it was still misty in there. We started on our tour, and one by one, all of our cameras stopped working; jammed shutters, newly charged batteries going flat – it was all very odd. One girl, called Catrina, managed to get a few snaps off in the area which looked like an Egyptian tomb

before her camera also stopped working. We developed all our own photos as part of the photography section of our degree course. Cat's photos had an old woman's face on the prints in different sizes and positions. We all found that to be very chilling. The woman had a blank look on her face. We told Cat to sell the photos, but she thought they were some sort of forewarning as she was very religious. I don't know what happened to the photos, but I don't think I'd want to see them again. I had about three photos from the visit showing the strange mist etc. … before my camera stopped working!

From Martin's description it is clear that the various camera problems which he and his fellow students experienced began shortly after they reached the Egyptian Avenue. That this area is so close to the spot where Joe Meek recorded what he considered to be a supernatural female voice, and that the resultant photographs appeared to show an elderly lady, is puzzling as no female ghosts have been sighted within Highgate Cemetery West to this author's knowledge. The ghost of a 'mad old woman', whom we shall meet in Chapter 3, does allegedly haunt the East Cemetery, however. Perhaps like the tall, dark figure she gets itchy feet once in a while!

The Ghost Interrupts a Guided Tour

From the survey of sightings of a tall, dark figure so far, it appears that, in common with the majority of 'ghosts', this apparition only manifests to one and sometimes two witnesses at any given time. A rare exception to this rule is recounted by Patricia Langley, author of *The Highgate Vampire Casebook* (2010). In 2004, Langley was one of approximately twenty visitors enjoying a tour of Highgate Cemetery West. Towards the conclusion of the tour, the group were listening to their guide in the most northerly section of the cemetery, at the juncture of two paths. Gazing around them as the guide pointed out various tombs and memorials, five of the party glanced down the track which leads to the cemetery's North Gate. They were bemused to observe a tall figure cloaked in black moving in the direction of the gate. As the guide indicated that it was time to return to the main gates, the witnesses remarked to him that they had not been made aware that the cemetery employed actors to enhance their tours. Langley recalls that the guide became immediately uncomfortable, and after curtly confirming that they did no such thing, rapidly ushered the group away from the top gate. As they exited into Swains Lane, Langley was able to ask the five visitors what they had seen on the path. They could only describe it as a tall man wearing some kind of cloak, who had disappeared whilst their attention was returned to the guide's lecture. They had assumed that this 'actor' had hidden amongst the shrubs and trees which border the path in an attempt to frighten them. While there are often gardeners and groundsmen to be found in the cemetery, it is common sense to assume that they do not wear cloaks, and as previously mentioned, entry to the locked cemetery by the public is strictly upon paid admission.

The reputedly haunted path which leads towards the North Gate, photographed from within the cemetery. (© Lorcan Maguire)

A Spectral Incursion at a Youth Hostel

As discussed in Chapter 1, whether or not the hooded and top-hatted spectres described by so many witnesses are one and the same is open to conjecture. This seems set to remain the case until such a time as they are encountered simultaneously. Regardless of this conundrum, the cowled entity seen through the cemetery gates and around the Circle of Lebanon also exhibits a propensity for travel.

A personal encounter with a hooded entity in the environs of Highgate Cemetery comes from a Mr Brendan Smyth, now of Edenfield in Lancashire but originally from Northern Ireland. At some stage between the summer of 1968 and early 1970, when in his mid-teens, Mr Smyth had moved to England with relatives, and was staying temporarily at the YHA's Highgate hostel, located at 84 West Hill. West Hill is, as its name suggests, a steep ascent on the western side of the village, which curls tightly around the cemetery's boundaries. Opened in 1936, some thirty-five years later the hostel (which closed in 1997) was not just a bolthole for young backpackers but a base for transient families making their first inroads into a new life in London. To this end it provided a shared kitchen occupying most of the top floor, which was big enough to allow the several families lodging there to eat and socialise together. Then a young man in a strange country, with no knowledge of local ghost stories, Brendan remembers that this particular room (at least 40 feet above the garden below) overlooked the wall which borders the north-west edge of the cemetery, at a distance of approximately 100 yards.

One weekday evening Brendan recalls that he was watching television when he felt hungry, and went to the communal kitchen to cook some Vesta chicken. As he was eating, he suddenly felt a chill run through him. Turning and looking up to the kitchen window above the sink, a window which he recalls being approximately 5 feet wide and 7 feet high, he was astonished to see through the glass a darkly cloaked figure with an illuminated, circular face, rising upwards in a slow but deliberate fashion. As Brendan reflects today: 'You know how some people say that the room goes cold when there's a ghost or something there? Nonsense. It's the feeling you get from your subconscious when something or someone's looking at you that makes you realise and turn round.'

Although it bore no discernible facial features, the apparition's black hood was wrapped around a glowing, orangey-yellow visage, which seemed to be staring at him with invisible eyes. Alone, and frozen with fear, Brendan watched for five to seven seconds as the figure continued to rise upwards to its full height, which was considerable. It then hovered, before passing through the window pane into the kitchen. As it emerged into clear view, Brendan noticed that the black figure faded somewhere in the region of where the lower torso should have been. It had no feet, and Brendan remembers vividly feeling transfixed as it moved in an eerily focused direction towards him ...

Suddenly, the spell somehow broken (he presumes by pure terror), Brendan leapt to his feet and ran screaming to the hallway, where he was met by two other male tenants, including a Scotsman named Jim. Both laughed at him, presuming 'the Irish guy' must be

The Youth Hostel at West Hill, photographed in the early 1970s, the same period when a whole room of lodgers claim to have seen a hooded spectre enter a top-floor window. (© Hampstead-Heath.net)

drunk, and didn't believe him. For days afterwards Brendan was the subject of mockery, but this was soon to change.

One evening approximately a week later, Jim and his English wife, Celia, were playing cards in the kitchen with three other tenants and Brendan's sister Pearl. Brendan was not present. Suddenly something drew Celia and Pearl's attention towards the window, causing them both to scream. Turning around, the other tenants were horrified to see the same apparition rising at window level, above the kitchen sink which Brendan had seen previously. The six witnesses promptly ran out the room, and it was not until the next day that Jim had calmed down enough to describe their encounter to Brendan and, with reference to the ribbing they had subjected him to, apologised with: 'We're sorry for laughing.'

Soon after this Brendan and his family moved out of the hostel, and put the experience behind them. Some forty-three years after these events the uncanny, almost robotic movement of the apparition, coupled with its lack of facial features, remains most strongly imprinted upon Mr Smyth's memory. He has no theories as to why this strange entity appeared to be trying to communicate with him and the other residents, and is glad that this did not come to pass. Even as a cynic regarding the 'otherside', he offers no explanation for these experiences as anything other than a truthful record of something which he does not understand, and has no desire to experience again.

'Elemental Forces' from Highgate Cemetery

A decade previously, and less than a quarter of a mile from the youth hostel, another household also experienced spectral incursions in the vicinity of Highgate Cemetery West. Whatever the nature of the entity or entities which seem to emanate from within the cemetery, their aerial faculties are a recurrent theme for, again, this account describes encounters which took place at the top of the house. Mr Raymond Irons, originally from Wales but of Cornish ancestry, is a professional photographer with an intimidating CV which includes a stint in the late 1960s as sub-editor of the popular weekly trivia magazine *TitBits*. Under a pen name he has also published several books about psychic self-defence – a subject which he

first began studying in earnest shortly after moving into 31 Langbourne Mansions on Highgate's Holly Lodge Estate in 1960.

Positioned within tall mock-Tudor mansion blocks built in the 1920s, the flats which comprise much of this exclusive and gated community are deceptively small, having been built for single women who had moved to London to gain clerical employment. Langbourne Mansions was the first terrace to be constructed, on land once belonging to the grounds of a villa built in 1798 by Sir Henry Tempest, but better known as the home of Victorian socialite and philanthropist Angela Burdett-Coutts of the famous banking dynasty. With its fantastic aerial views of Highgate and the adjacent East Cemetery, Ray's flat today has a light and pleasant atmosphere, although the presence of various protective occult symbols above the doors suggests that this was not always the case.

When Ray and his wife first moved into the flat, he was swiftly and somewhat rudely alerted to the possibility that all was not right on the Holly Lodge Estate. One night, having taken refuge on the sitting-room sofa after a minor domestic, Ray was awoken by the sound of what he describes as three 'masculine energy forms' rushing into the flat. As he pulled the bedclothes over his head to avoid their gaze, Ray heard the sound of heavy breathing, as if the intruders were leaning over him. 'They came to look at me. They weren't ghosts,' Ray insists. 'I'd seen ghosts before and could tell the difference. They were elemental forces.' After a while the trio rushed out through the bathroom, the window banging open as they did so. Ray's flat is on the fourth floor.

Langbourne Mansions, where Ray Irons claims his top-floor flat was invaded by elemental forces in 1960. (© Dave Milner)

After this incident the flat became, in Ray's words, like Piccadilly Circus. Doors would slam of their own accord and books would fly from shelves. But always this destruction seemed to occur in the wake of some invisible force which would charge about the flat, entering through the bathroom window and exiting through the same or the front door – having the courtesy to open each but not to close them behind it.

A frightening incident forced Ray to conclude that something had to be done about conditions in the flat. 'There are things in the cemetery,' he claims, 'which come out and attack people.' One night as he lay reading in bed, with his wife asleep next to him, he heard a kind of twittering sound, and felt the distinct impression that something had moved through the bedroom wall and 'flopped' on to his chest. Unable to breath or move, and convinced that he was not experiencing sleep paralysis, Ray summoned all the strength he could, and, as he puts it, 'calling on a Higher Power', blasted the negative force out of him with a violent exhalation of breath. This turn of events led to a lifelong fascination with ways in which people who are apparently especially psychically sensitive can protect themselves from 'lower astral and other dark influences'. Today, wherever he is, Ray says that he feels surrounded by a protective force. 'Now none can come to me in my flat. I have set up a protective barrier,' he states with great self-assurance. His books on this subject, borne as he puts it out of a personal necessity to shield his home and family from their unearthly neighbours, continue to receive glowing reviews today.

Romano—Celtic Hooded Spirits in North London

In his 2012 opus *Quest for the Hexham Heads*, folklorist Paul Screeton revived interest in the concept of the Romano-Celtic godforms referred to as *genii cucullati*, or 'hooded spirits'. Many stone icons representing *genii cucullati* have been uncovered and catalogued by archaeologists across Europe since the 1930s, when the cult was formally named. In Britain these tend to show hooded male spirits in triplicate (such a relief discovered in London is now housed in the British Museum), while on the continent they are depicted standing alone. The carving of three deities could simply be an emphasis of the power attributed to one deity, as was common practice amongst the Celts. In both depictions the deities are always swathed in the full-length cloaks with conical hoods from which their name derives, and these artefacts have often been found near ancient springs and other venerated water sources. It is certainly true that the many streams which now run beneath the cemetery and Swains Lane date back to antiquity, and would have been visible to our Celtic and Roman ancestors.

We will never know if these 'hooded spirits' were actually seen by Ancient Britons, or if they were simply representations of conceptual godforms. Paranormal historian M.J.Wayland noted in 2012 that the proliferation of sightings of hooded figures in the Cotswolds and Northumbria corresponds with the discovery of anomalous numbers of stone *genii cucullati* in these areas. He also postulates that 'with black monks we are either dealing with archaic spirits that form our haunted countryside or they could be an inbuilt folk memory that is replayed after the "trigger effect" that starts the paranormal experience.'

With no monastery nearby which could account for the ghostly appearance of hooded figures in the vicinity of Highgate Cemetery, and a Roman settlement in nearby Highgate Woods discovered in the 1960s, could Ray's otherworldly visitors have been exactly what he interpreted them to be – some form of elemental spirits? Although Ray has never seen the hooded spectre himself, examination of centuries-old carvings of *genii cucullati* reveals a striking resemblance to the figure which Michael Quinn and his colleague claim to have seen rising upwards behind the cemetery wall in 1962.

While some may regard Ray Irons' views with reservation, perhaps he is right to suggest that much alleged supernatural activity can only be properly examined with an awareness of a 'sense of place'. In a location of such historical significance and habitation as Highgate, the relationship between people and the environment will always be complex and inextricable. One of the most striking aspects of Highgate seems to be that the land, along with the natural and manmade features which define it, exists almost as a living participant itself. The many local history societies which thrive in Highgate and Hornsey are testament to the loyalty and co-dependence which for centuries have joined mankind and location, and influenced the evolution of both.

It is not just residents who partake of this extraordinary nod to a less globalised past. The hundreds of comments placed by visitors to Highgate Cemetery on websites such as TripAdvisor.com are indicative of its absorbing atmosphere. It seems that the highly immersive experience of a morning or afternoon spent touring the cemetery never fails to create a deep and lasting impact. From the moment one leaves The Colonnade and ventures into the quiet, tomb-strewn vales, one intuits strongly that this is an ancient and sacred place, which almost exists outside of time. The physical environment inevitably plays a role in this bombardment of the senses, with the lives and stories of those who have gone before lending the impression that they are imprinted upon the landscape itself.

A Seventeenth-Century Suspect

We will probably never know for sure whether the lonesome spectre which haunts Swains Lane and the West Cemetery is or ever was human, let alone confirm his name. There is one figure from history, however, who perhaps experienced more sorrow in connection with the land upon which Highgate Cemetery was built than any other. Interestingly, William Blake, who was born around 1630, has emotive connections with six key areas around the cemetery where a darkly-garbed entity has been witnessed. He also held familial links with Elisha Coysh, the plague doctor who occupied the cottage on Swains Lane during both of their lifetimes. Blake (an unproven ancestor of the metaphysical poet and artist of the same name) was a woollen draper and

vintner, who in his youth 'lived under the sign of The Golden Boy at Maidenlane, Covent Garden' (William Blake, 'Silver Drops, or Serious Things', c. 1670). Tragically, his wife Mary appears to have died young, leaving him to raise their infant sons alone.

In an attempt to distract himself from his grief, over the next forty years Blake developed a destructive obsession with the houses and land which fall away down Highgate's West Hill from South Grove. This began soon after he moved into the 'banqueting house', which was later to become Ashurst House. The grounds were laid out in an identical style to Ashurst's, with the Circle of Lebanon comprising Blake's private garden, and what is now the approach to St Michael's church forming his drive. It was here that one November night in 1985 a Mrs Janet Morrell reported seeing a tall, shadowy form disappear as it approached what would once have been the gates to the old house. Entrances to the estate, now the main and top gates of Highgate Cemetery, would also have been well-used by Blake.

Whilst seated upon what are now the Terrace Catacombs, gazing across London, Blake described hearing a 'calling' from God Himself. Perhaps influenced by the sadness experienced by his own motherless children, Blake decided that is was God's plan that a school should be built on the land, for orphaned boys and girls from Highgate and the surrounding parishes. His philanthropy placed him ahead of his time in many ways, but Blake also had an eccentric and reckless streak. Unable to fund this project himself, and in lieu of pennies falling from heaven, he decided that it was God's desire that the influential cabal

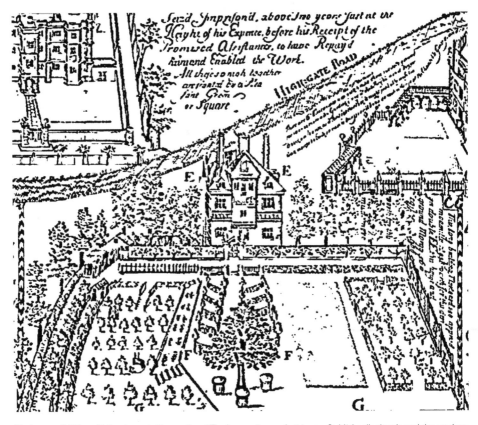

The home of William Blake, drawn in his own hand. The house sits on what is now St Michael's church, and the gardens shown are now occupied by the Circle of Lebanon. (Author's collection)

of landowners (including Sir William Ashurst) who owned the houses which he had earmarked for this project were morally bound to invest. They did so, but deployed methods which left Blake unable to pay the mortgages proffered.

Blake built a new house on the site around 1674, and at various times did manage to acquire and utilise Dorchester House for his orphanage, which sat a stone's throw away from the youth hostel previously discussed. Blake also purchased – and lost – The Flask public house on two occasions, where the shade of a brooding elderly gentleman in Jacobean clothing has been sighted, and it is here that Blake's property trans-actions would have been conducted,

during the petty sessions of the manorial court. Blake was sentenced at least twice to the Fleet debtors' prison as a result of these wrangles, but in the grip of a reli-gious mania remained undeterred from performing 'God's work'. Sir William Ashurst's acquisition via the bankruptcy court of Blake's house and garden, however, broke his spirit, and while the circumstances of Blake's death are vague, it is likely that he died during a third incarceration in the Fleet not long after 1687, dreaming of his much-loved, and eventually lost, house at Highgate. His final resting place is unknown.

Could the figure seen peering through the bars of Highgate Cemetery be Blake, still jealously protecting 'his' land? If so, the YHA's use of 84 West Hill could certainly have attracted his attention. As a militant Protestant, Blake may also have lent his approval to the construction of the cemetery, and certainly to St Michael's church, which could explain the lacuna of sightings of the figure in black between this time and the cemetery's fall into ruin. Conversely, by the late 1960s, Pagan and black magic rituals, vandalism, and modern developments upon what he saw as a site favoured by God, would certainly have aroused the ire of this embittered character who, despite his grand vision, remains a mere footnote in Highgate's history.

3

HIGHGATE CEMETERY EAST

By 1853, over 10,000 people had been laid to rest in Highgate Cemetery. In notable contrast to William Allingham's lines from his 1850 poem 'In Highgate Cemetery':

> Yet, 'neath the universal sky,
> Bright children here too run and sing,
> Calm verdure waxes green and high,
> And grave-side roses smell of Spring.

Goldthorn Hill, writing in *The Ladies Companion* in 1861, graphically bemoans the olfactory impact of this unnatural scale of internment:

> Of Highgate I scarcely like to speak; for who desires to speak ill of that which they have once well loved? and yet, on most warm days, the exhalations from the gratings in Swains Lane have made us reel with faintness, and, for all the wealth of flowers and their perfume, the digging of a grave makes itself evident from one end of a walk to the other, so saturated is the soil with the malaria of decay.

The burial of so many bodies, often diseased, upon the slopes of Highgate's West Hill, was soon to take its toll upon London's already unsanitary drinking water. Although Highgate is situated upon an intricate grid of underground watercourses, its access to these had always been intermittent and inadequate, and now even these were to become imbibed with the very essence of death. In his 1859 *Plea For Free Drinking Fountains In The Metropolis*, E.T. Wakefield observed that the shallow well water of London's pumps 'receives the drainage of Highgate Cemetery which percolates the soil on the London side of the Cemetery, and flows towards the Metropolis', and that a man who 'habitually makes use of London pump water lives in perpetual danger of disease. The carbonic acid of the decomposed matter makes them sparkling, and the nitrates they contain give them a pleasant coolness to the taste.'

Wakefield's nauseating ruminations upon 'the hideous reality of the survivors of each generation immediately drinking in solution the mortal remains of their predecessors' were published just five years after the London Cemetery Company decided to acquire 19 acres of land on the east side of Swains Lane on which to further expand the burgeoning necropolis. The official and suitably noble motivation for this decision was the social duty to provide additional burial plots for London's booming population. As we have seen, however, providing space for London's dead had proved to be a very lucrative venture.

Opened for business in 1860, the East Cemetery could in many ways be seen as a poor country cousin to Highgate Cemetery West. To save the indignity of funeral processions being forced to cross muddy Swains Lane, in 1855 a tunnel was dug between the two cemeteries. The tunnel enabled coffins, lowered with the use of a hydraulic catafalque situated in the chapel, to be transported discreetly whilst remaining on (or in) consecrated ground. This innovation aside, the East Cemetery's comparative lack of ground-level tombs seems to have saved it from the ravages of vandalism to which its next-door neighbour has been subject over the decades.

Like the old cemetery, the East Cemetery is not free to visit, although visitors are allowed to deviate from the guided tour, and admission costs approximately half the price. This impression of it being a pauper's alternative extends to its lack of ghostly residents; indeed it seems that in Highgate even the wandering dead like to keep up with the Joneses. Throughout the many years during which this author has researched countless reports of alleged supernatural goings-on in and around Highgate, not one has been forthcoming which claims

The imposing gates of Highgate Cemetery East. (© Lorcan Maguire)

an actual sighting of an entity of any kind in Highgate Cemetery East. The sole exception to this rule is found in the conclusion of Martin Trent's account detailed in Chapter 1.

In 1971, renowned folklore expert Eric Maple visited Highgate Cemetery in person to investigate the reports of occult-related vandalism and paranormal activity which were by now common in mainstream media. He published the findings of his enquiries, during which he interviewed many local people, that same year in an article for esoteric magazine *Man, Myth and Magic*. Maple recounts:

> Not surprisingly, Highgate Cemetery has a ghost, a solitary spectre which has been seen at night standing close to the huge iron entrance gates, gazing motionlessly into space. Little is known about it, but this ghost, like the vampire, has its devotees; there is an old gentleman who always asks about it, and an elderly lady who is said to commune with it.

Drawing upon Maple's published research, Peter Underwood in his book *Haunted London* (1973) transposes local people's experiences of this apparition to Highgate Cemetery East. The additional flourishes which Underwood appears to lend to the ghost's attributes have perhaps irrevocably distorted popular understanding of the appearance and behaviour of the entity. In what has become an incredibly widely circulated account (ironically often not credited to Underwood himself but repeated ad infinitum as 'fact'), the 'solitary spectre', as it is still referred to, has now been afforded 'bony fingers' – but at least it is still 'reported to linger in the vicinity of the huge iron gates'. The wrong gates,

however … Also, perplexingly, the spectre is now described as a 'white shrouded figure' – the first and only time we read an account which describes any gate-lurking entity as wearing any colour other than black, or dark grey. True to Maple's account, the figure still 'seems to gaze pensively into space', but it has unaccountably become 'oblivious to human beings until they approach too close [when] it suddenly disappears, only to appear a short distance away, adopting the same listless gaze'. Underwood does, however, retain Maple's original (and first-hand) observation that 'there are those who claim to have communicated with the passive phantom'.

In conclusion, it seems that the ubiquitous figure which loiters around the gates of Highgate Cemetery West – and has possibly also been seen in Waterlow Park and as far afield as Cholmeley Park – has some aversion to Highgate Cemetery East.

A 'Mad Old Woman' Searching among the Graves

There is, however, one ghost who seems to be solely associated with the East Cemetery.

This spectral female also seems to have entered the printed pantheon of Highgate's legends courtesy of Peter Underwood. Again writing in *Haunted London*, Underwood alleges to have talked with 'two people who claim to have seen this ghost from different viewpoints at the same time, but always the fast-moving figure disappears from view before it can be closely studied and it always eludes those who try to follow it'. He continues: 'The ghost is thought to be an old and mad woman whose children were buried here after she had murdered them, and now her sad and restless spirit seeks the graves of those she harmed but really loved.'

Descriptions of this ghost, with her 'thin hair streaming behind her as she passes swiftly among the mouldering tombs', vary slightly in retellings, but an element which never alters is her association with children who at some time were in her care and who met with foul play. Underwood's report does not furnish the reader with any clues as to how the witnesses, or indeed Underwood himself, were aware of the 'mad old woman's' purported crimes. If there is any foundation to Underwood's report, a then extant oral tradition may explain this. There are two long-forgotten and extremely macabre incidents from Highgate's hidden history which might in turn shed light on this folk tale's origins. The first came to public attention on 8 January 1845. As the *Morning Chronicle* reported:

> as a number of boys were playing in the fields near the Highgate Cemetery, some of them proceeded to climb an old tree situate between Swains-lane and the upper part of Maiden-lane. Whilst thus engaged, one of the boys got into the tree's trunk, at the bottom of which he discovered a black bundle, which on being opened was found to contain the body of a child. The body was somewhat decomposed, but it is stated that the head is much bruised, and that there are other marks of violence on its person.

The location given for the hollow tree would place it, on a modern map, at the southern extremity of what is now the East Cemetery. As far as this author can ascertain, the crime was never solved, but news of the discovery would doubtless have spread quickly through Highgate Village and the wider community.

In August 1865 another gruesome and distressing discovery was made, this time in Green Dragon Alley, which linked North Grove and North Road behind The Green Dragon public house (now demolished). The Green Dragon was certainly not a salubrious establishment; it was here that body snatcher John Bishop would meet with fellow professional criminals some forty years previously to hatch his various schemes. That evening, a tailor by the name of Robert M. Pringle was making his way home when he stumbled upon a parcel carefully tied up with string, which he took home and opened in the presence of his family. To the horror of all present, as Pringle opened the parcel an infant's head rolled out on the table. The remaining contents contained the hideously mutilated and partial remains of a child aged approximately 10 days old, and an inquest into the death was held the following month at The Gatehouse public house. Amongst the evidence debated was the account of a witness who had seen two women approaching St Joseph's Retreat on Highgate Hill. The first woman was observed to repeatedly ask the second to help her carry a very young child as they walked, whilst the second passed the child back and tried to run away before being repeatedly entreated to take the child again. The relationship between these two women and why the child was brought to Highgate in the first place we shall never know. Frustratedly, the coroner concluded a verdict of wilful murder against a person or persons unknown

One of the paths in Highgate Cemetery East along which the ghost of a 'mad old woman' is said to dash, searching for her murdered children. (© Lorcan Maguire)

and the case was closed. Just seven years later a 'mangling shop' was discovered by the police to be operating out of an old house, in a secluded alley of Highgate. Its proprietors made their living by deliberately disfiguring children and adults so that they might command more pennies as professional beggars. Could there be a connection?

It is quite possible that the two murders recounted here, with the additional flavour of the two females witnessed struggling over a baby in the case of the second death, may have become conflated over time. The presumed 'murderess' becomes the killer of *two* innocent children despite the twenty-year gap between the killings, and becomes the local 'bogeywoman'. It is easy to imagine an 1860s or 1870s mother in Highgate warning a naughty child that 'the mad woman' would come and chop them up and put them in the hollow tree if they did not behave, and this threat being passed on from generation to generation. And so perhaps a legend is born, although sadly through the deaths of two innocents whose names we shall never know.

4

HAUNTED PUBLIC HOUSES

Public houses have played an important part in Highgate's development. By 1780 over eighty coaches a day were stopping in the village, and Highgate's role as a watering place for drovers and other travellers on the Great North Road meant that by 1826 there were no fewer than nineteen licensed premises. All of these possessed giant sets of stag or bullocks' horns, upon which visitors were made 'freemen of Highgate' during the ancient ceremony of 'Swearing on the Horns'. Two of the oldest surviving pubs from this period, The Gatehouse and The Flask, are fittingly the most haunted.

The Gatehouse

A predecessor of this large, mock–Tudor pub was first licensed in 1670, although a building had stood on this site since the 1300s, by which time a hermit was collecting tolls from travellers who wished to pass through this gateway into the Bishop of London's land. Not only does

The Gatehouse divide north from south, in the past it sat on the boundary of London and Middlesex, then the parishes of Hornsey and St Pancras, and, until recently, straddled Camden and Haringey councils' boundaries. Perhaps this long history of being 'in between' worlds has encouraged the many supernatural occurrences which are alleged to have taken place inside its ancient walls.

The Gatehouse public house, Highgate, at the busy junction of North Hill and Hampstead Lane. (© Dave Milner)

Old Mother Marnes
Frightens the Police

While The Gatehouse is reportedly home to several resident ghosts, the best known is certainly that of 'Mother Marnes', an unfortunate widow who was supposedly murdered for her money in the seventeenth century. From the 1970s onwards, when Mother Marnes's tragic tale found its way into the many popular collections of ghost stories which continue to reference Highgate, she was unfailingly described as clad in black widow's weeds, and accompanied by a cat. Her appearances are also limited in these repetitive accounts to occasions when no children or animals are present in the building. This proviso makes Mother Marnes a very unusual ghost, and rather suggests that the originating accounts of her manifestations have got lost somewhere in translation; traditionally, children are presumed to be more sensitive to the presence of 'ghosts' than adults, whilst animals often exhibit signs of fear and distress in situations where paranormal activity is suspected. Perhaps it is no surprise, then, that publicans and patrons of The Gatehouse who claim first-hand encounters with Mother Marnes, or know someone who does, describe her somewhat differently.

In 1965 Jack O'Connell, originally from County Kilkenny in south-east Ireland, became the latest in a long line of landlords employed by the Finch's chain of public houses to manage The Gatehouse. Jack, accompanied by his wife, six young children and their Jack Russell terrier 'Cappy', occupied the staff living quarters on the rear first floor of the pub, and initially warmed to their new home. In an interview with this author in 2014, Jack, who is now in his eighties, remembered his tenure in Highgate fondly, recalling amongst other happy memories his friendship with John Betjeman, one of the village's most beloved residents, with whom he spent many pleasant hours at the boating lake in Hyde Park.

Shortly after the family had settled into The Gatehouse, however, the three older children, then aged 9, 10 and 11, began telling their parents about what they described as 'a lady in a grey dress with a big hat' standing in their bedrooms at night. This mysterious woman seemed particularly fond of Jack's daughter Deirdre, who often saw the figure enter her room and stand at the foot of the bed, as if she wished to guard her in her sleep. Soon the figure, observed only by the children, was also appearing in daylight, gliding through the many rooms and corridors on the first floor. One afternoon she was even seen by the oldest boy Desmond, gazing into what was then the ballroom – apparently standing or hovering outside on the 4in-wide window ledge. It should be noted that the ballroom was substantially remodelled in 1890 and previously extended slightly further north than the present dimensions, although it is unlikely that 11-year-old Desmond would have known this.

With no reason to disbelieve the children, who were not at all perturbed by their new friend, Jack questioned them more closely about the figure's attire, and was able to ascertain that she seemed to be dressed in costume popular in England in the early 1600s, adorning the wide-brimmed style of hat which was common around this time. Sadly it seems that any records which could have established Mother Marnes's identity have been lost to time, which, given the often transient nature of those who have lodged, lived or died in Highgate's many hostelries, is unsurprising. However, we do know that in 1682 one 'Widow Barnes', formally known as Judith Barnes, owned land adjacent to The Gatehouse. This could suggest a possible candidate, or at least that one of Judith's marital ancestors could explain the popular adoption of the similar-sounding surname 'Marnes'.

It was around a month later that Jack, his wife and their head barman Tom Brady began hearing overhead footsteps whilst serving in the bar. Tom, who lived out and was unaware of the children's nightly visitor, had previously mooted to Jack that he thought the pub might be haunted as 'nothing ever stays put in this house!' The footfalls, which were heard only when the children were away from home, at school or asleep at night, were light, and always seemed to traverse from the flat to what was then a small catering kitchen. For fear of ridicule, no mention was made of the footsteps to anyone outside the household. Soon enough, however, on one occasion when the sounds were clearly audible during pub opening hours, they became impossible to ignore. The regulars – who calmly insisted that they were accustomed to hearing the sounds – remained to Jack's astonishment entirely relaxed about the inhuman noises above their heads.

Inevitably Jack and Tom quickly became the butt of the regulars' good-humoured jokes, and wagers even began to be placed about how long the new tenants could 'stick it out'. Suspecting that the villagers may have written them off as 'superstitious Irishmen' who were easily frightened, Jack consulted a less humorously inclined neighbour whose house backed on to the pub itself. Grudgingly, the neighbour confirmed that the pub and adjacent outbuildings and flats were genuinely considered by locals to have several spectral occupants. These included a man or two men in the pub's basement, and a woman in grey known as 'Mother Marnes' – although no one could remember when or why she had acquired this name. Local opinion was divided upon whether the ghost was the victim of a murder which took place in The Gatehouse itself, or the subject of a corrupt murder trial which took place on the premises, in the days when trials and inquests were held in the old courtroom. That the courtroom is located on the ground floor, where Mother Marnes has never been sighted, suggests that the latter is unlikely. This confusion was exacerbated by the fact that no one born and bred in Highgate, according to Jack's neighbour, could recall a time when they were not aware of the ghostly legends associated with The Gatehouse, and Highgate in general. Jack recalls that this gentleman was also under the impression that some members of the Highgate Scientific and Literary Institution, whose headquarters have been based at the same premises in Highgate Village since 1839, had once commissioned a study of Highgate's ghosts, so common were supernatural 'sightings' in the area.

The 1973 classic British horror film *The Wicker Man* would not be released for another eight years, but one can imagine Jack's bemusement unfolding when, as a stranger in town, he learned of the beliefs which many of his neighbours upheld regarding the peculiarities of their isolated suburb.

One night, after approximately a year's residence at The Gatehouse, Jack and Tom were enjoying a quiet drink in the bar an hour or so after last orders, Mrs O'Connell, the children and the dog enjoying a short break away. It is not improbable that contemporary reportage by the BBC and the *Daily Mail* of the events of that night contributed to the earlier-mentioned assertion that Mother Marnes will not manifest when animals and children are present. Indeed, the reports in question do seem to be the first on public record which make direct reference to Mother Marnes.

Jack recalls that suddenly, around midnight, the pub's calm atmosphere was disturbed by a loud knocking on the main door. The unexpected guests proved to be two police officers, professing their concern that the bar being dimly lit, with its closed curtains, may have indicated the presence of burglars. Aware not only of the officers' probable desire for a late night drink, but also of an increase in the inexplicable sounds in recent days, Jack seized an opportunity to surreptitiously engage two credible witnesses. As fortune would have it, a short time after the four men had settled down with their drinks, the now common sound of unaccountable footsteps from the ceiling commenced in earnest, tracing as usual a path from the flat to the kitchen. This time the footsteps culminated in odd bangings, suggesting the sounds of a struggle.

After a swift discussion it was agreed that, as the kitchen had two entrances via staircases at opposite ends of the bar, it should be approached severally. Accordingly, Jack and a somewhat trepidatious Tom ascended the two staircases, each accompanied by a police officer. As the parties approached the kitchen, both heavy oaken doors which were closed, all distinctly heard the sounds of female and male voices raised as if in argument, and what they took to be the clattering of the sharp knives in the cutlery drawer. After a long and tense pause, both teams threw open the doors almost simultaneously, at which juncture the policemen found themselves brandishing their truncheons at each other. The kitchen was devoid of human occupancy, with no signs of disturbance, and an embarrassed and rapid return to the comfort of the bar ensued – with the police at the helm.

Was the spirit of Mother Marnes, devoid of the company of the children she so diligently watched over each night, disturbed by the policemen's talk of burglary? And could this have triggered an interrupted replay of a fateful night so many years ago? Not wishing to worry his young family, Jack told no one of these strange events, and was surprised to be contacted just days later by the national press. It seems that 'ten pound a tip' was the going rate in the 1960s for a newsworthy story, a sum perhaps not considered beneath some of the local constabulary. Reports about the incident attracted the attention of the Society for Psychical Research, which dispatched an enthusiastic team of paranormal investigators, begging to be locked in the pub overnight with various kinds of equipment. 'For the craic', as he remembers it, Jack fulfilled their wishes, but to the disappointment of all the ghost did little more than drop the mercury a few times, and refused to put in an appearance – rather like Mother Marnes's alleged feline companion!

Mother Marnes's Missing Cat

Out of all the interviews with actual witnesses to Mother Marnes that this author has conducted, none mentions the presence of a cat. Perhaps this addition to the legend finds its origins in the popular association between Highgate and Dick Whittington's cat, which is represented to this day by a sculpture on Highgate Hill. Gruesomely, a mummified cat with an equally skeletal rat was displayed in the window of the nearby Whittington and Cat public house for many years in the early part of the nineteenth century, having been found in the chimney during building work. The cat and mouse can still be seen at the back of this pub, which holidaymakers to Highgate would doubtless have made their first port of call after passing through the tollgate at the bottom of the hill. Most of these jaunts inevitably included a visit to The Gatehouse, where tourists were 'sworn at Highgate' and may also have been regaled with tales of Mother Marnes. If this long-dead cat was the inspiration for Mother Marnes's elusive pet, this could help date some of the oral tradition associated with her.

A centuries-old cat and accompanying rat, discovered in the late seventeenth century during renovations to the Whittington and Cat public house on Highgate Hill. Presumed to be a classic 'house guardian' sacrifice, the cat was found within the chimney breast, and was for many years displayed in the window and until 2014 in a glass case. Could this long-deceased cat have inspired the legend of Mother Marnes's ghostly feline companion, associated with The Gatehouse? © Jessica Chilton

The ghost's aversion to animals also seems unfounded, as Jack O'Connell's small dog was present in The Gatehouse during the majority of Mother Marnes's manifestations, although like the children he remained nonplussed. 'If that ghost had a cat, Cappy would have been right in there,' laughs Jack.

A Seventeenth-Century Burglar on the Prowl

In the summer of 1966, unworried by the ghost but disenchanted with Highgate, the O'Connell family moved to a different pub in Chelsea. If the seemingly soothing presence of the O'Connells' children decreased the most extreme replays of Mother Marnes's murder in The Gatehouse, just three months after their departure, there is some suggestion that the situation had reverted to form.

In October 1966 a male apparition was spotted by a Mr Tony Abbott, who was listening to a jazz band perform in the ballroom area of the pub. Seeking the public telephone, he left his friends and wandered the nearby darkened corridors, entering rooms at random. Turning a corner, Mr Abbott was startled to see a tall man striding down the hallway before him. What confused Mr Abbot more than the figure's sudden appearance, and the fact that he was wearing a cape and a 'Guy Fawkes' type hat, was the strange man's ability to pass through a closed door.

Against his better judgement, and motivated by a trance-like compulsion which he did not understand, Mr Abbott followed the stranger, and found himself alone in an obviously disused room with a bell tower-shaped ceiling. Unnerved, he maintains that he turned to leave but was overcome by a rushing sound, and a feeling of icy coldness. Within seconds these odd conditions had escalated to an intense experience of suffocation, as if Mr Abbott was being violently smothered by some invisible assailant. Although he survived the 1966 incident with minimal physical injuries, Mr Abbott did not discuss it with anyone until many decades later.

Some years ago a framed compilation of ghost stories associated with The Gatehouse hung in the bar downstairs, until it vanished overnight – presumably having been stolen by souvenir hunters. One of those stories told of an American tourist who, in 1963, saw a woman in grey hanging out of a window as if crying for help, on the same floor and side of the building that Tony Abbott found himself lost in. Could the seventeenth-century figure he encountered be the shade of the burglar who assaulted – and then perhaps silenced forever – a screaming Mother Marnes?

'Landlord George Sees a Ghost'

Despite being unaware of Tony Abbott's traumatic experience, the O'Connells' successor lasted just four months before complaining to Finch's that the pub was haunted and obtaining a transfer. At this time The Gatehouse was one of the most lucrative public houses in North London and recruiting a replacement manager was a speedy process. By early December, George Sample, 52 years of age and with thirty-one years' experience in the pub trade, had taken over. He was accompanied by his wife Mafalda and their long-time head barman Rodney Andrew.

Perhaps Mother Marnes is particular about whom she is willing to share her home with, as according to the *Ham & High* by January 1967 George Sample had experienced two nerve-wracking encounters with an aggressive entity on the balcony above the ballroom, which resulted in his admission to the local Whittington hospital. To make things worse, Rodney Andrew subsequently had the displeasure of a near identical experience, culminating in a violent fall down the connecting flight of stairs. According to Mr Sample:

> It started on a Tuesday only a few days after we arrived. At midnight I had to go up to the gallery, above the ballroom, to turn out the lights. As I switched the last light out this thing appeared. I'll never forget it. It had a very old, wrinkled face – impossible to tell if it was a man or a woman – with grey hair parted down the middle, and it was wearing a black smock. It floated just clear of the ground and leered at me. I said 'What do you want?', but there was no reply. I rushed downstairs and next morning I collapsed and was taken to hospital. I came back against my doctor's orders.

It is interesting that Mr Sample's encounter took place in one of the oldest parts of The Gatehouse, within yards of the kitchen area which forms the core of the original structure.

Like the O'Connells, the Samples were treated to locked and bolted doors opening by themselves, and many of Mother Marnes's aural demonstrations, with Mrs Sample quoted as saying: 'I hate the place – I can't wait to get out of it. My daughter visited us once, heard the footsteps, and said she would never come again.'

A few days later, Mr Sample had another encounter with the ghost. 'It was exactly the same as before, only this time it spoke,' he said. 'I again said: "What do you want?" and it said, "You are taking him with you." That was all.' Whatever its meaning, the apparition's cryptic utterance certainly pre-empted the Samples' departure less than two months after moving into The Gatehouse – along with that of Rodney Andrew. The relief manager who took over from the Samples allegedly refused to live on the premises. Whether he also had an unpleasant experience in the pub is unrecorded; however, Finch's appeal for a permanent manager in the *Morning Advertiser* would hardly have calmed his fears. It contained the caveat: 'This house is reputed to be haunted.'

The Ghost of a Smuggler

Sample's and Andrew's experiences were not unique, as we learn from an article from the *Daily Telegraph* of 3 September 1947. It recounts that, like Sample, then landlord Brian Harvey was admitted to hospital 'suffering from shock after claiming to have seen a ghost'. From the fact that well-known medium Trixie Allingham is cited in the same article as having (presumably subsequently) visited The Gatehouse and found the gallery to be a 'cold, evil place', we can infer with some degree of probability that this was also the site of Harvey's encounter. Trixie claimed to psychically intuit that the 'ghost' was that of a 'white haired smuggler, who was murdered on the premises after an argument over money'.

A little-known fact about The Gatehouse may support Trixie's assertions about a smuggler having cause to visit the hostelry. A rare book, published in 1919 with the aid of private subscriptions and titled simply *Highgate Village*, reveals that in 1912 a secret room was discovered behind the fireplace of one of the downstairs rooms adjoining the Masonic banqueting hall. This snippet of local knowledge has never made its way into more widely circulated histories of Highgate, and was remembered personally by the book's author Walter Savage, who was a long-term editor of the *Ham & High*. Graffiti revealed at the time with the date 1706 suggests that the secret room, which was certainly large enough to store a decent supply of smuggled goods, sits within part of the oldest remnants of the original building.

More Disturbances in the Ballroom

In 1976 Andrew Hubbard was 14 years old, and was confined to The Gatehouse in the evenings while his mother acted as relief manager. Being under age, he was told to stay on the balcony out the way of the grown-ups. He recalls:

> The large old fashioned electricity box turned off (this was about 8 feet from me). All of the lights went out and after a minute or so my mother appeared and threw the handle on the box to 'on'. As soon as she had done this I saw the handle slowly move back up unaided and all power tripped off again. A little too young to understand or be spooked, I reset

the handle myself after my mother ran away screaming! I was later told that other incidents had occurred, including all of the chandeliers in the ballroom swinging wildly while a young barman was stocking the bar prior to opening time.

A Haunted Theatre and a Ghost with a Shoe Fetish

By the early 1990s the pub's ownership had changed, and with it its fortune. For some years it was boarded up and unoccupied, until after a complicated set of negotiations the Wetherspoons pub chain acquired the ground floor and staff quarters and Ovation Theatres Ltd took over the ballroom area, former kitchen and adjacent rooms. Ovation's co-founder John Plews takes a pragmatic approach to Mother Marnes's presence in his theatre, and encourages actors to treat her with respect – lest they lose their shoes! In an interview with this author, John was insistent that many actors as recently as 2013 have found themselves frantically searching for missing shoes in the dressing room. Interestingly, this area is located directly upon the trajectory of the footsteps which were so frequently heard in the 1960s. It seems that the shoes are regularly borrowed and later returned by what John considers to be a relatively amicable ghost.

Things weren't always so easy-going though. In 1993, when John was waiting to sign the final paperwork, only the landlord was allowed a key to the property. This afforded Ovation no access to the building after office hours, leaving John concerned and perplexed when he began to receive complaints from residents of the adjacent flats about the sounds of a heavy object being 'shuffled' or 'dragged about' at just after 3 a.m. Complaints continue intermittently to this day as different tenants come and go, despite no one sleeping in the theatre's allocated rooms. Additionally, many Wetherspoons employees have reported minor poltergeist activity in the two staff flats which adjoin the theatre, although the present occupants have experienced no problems. Around 1994, a burglar alarm system was installed in what is now a successful theatre known as Upstairs at the Gatehouse. One particular sensor, located in the theatre close to the balcony steps, was repeatedly triggered at exactly 3.a.m. Tests and replacement devices provided by the security firm which installed the system provided no clues as to what was triggering the sensor in this particular location, and eventually it was permanently disabled.

John recalls other odd incidents which occurred in 1993. One evening, while carrying out an inspection of Ovation's renovations to what would eventually become the box office, the managing agent locked the door to the north stairwell behind him brusquely. He was extremely unnerved to hear several loud and distinct raps on the other side of the door, despite being alone in the building. Had he inadvertently slammed the door in Mother Marnes's face? The door, no longer present, was the same door which was flung open by an equally perturbed off-duty police officer in 1966.

The haunted gallery above the old ballroom in The Gatehouse. The gallery now overlooks the auditorium of the popular theatre 'Upstairs at the Gatehouse', and is used by lighting technicians. (© Dave Milner)

The heavy and stiff 'on/off' trip switch on the balcony in The Gatehouse, which Andrew Hubbard saw move by itself in 1976. (© Dave Milner)

Around this time a heavy bench, some 7 feet long and 1½ feet wide, was left one afternoon in the middle of the ballroom. The next morning it was discovered 15 yards away, pushed neatly against the northern wall. This bench now supports the mixing desk for the theatre's lighting and sound rigs, and can be found on the allegedly haunted balcony where incidents of electrical malfunction still occasionally occur. In situ is the still-functioning 'old fashioned electricity box' mentioned by Andrew Hubbard, complete with its huge 'ON/OFF' handle and plate dated 1963. In true theatrical tradition, electrical faults these days are usually solved by asking the ghost politely to 'stop mucking about'.

Over the last twenty years many paranormal groups have carried out nocturnal vigils in the theatre, with inconclusive results. Unlike the many actors who have trod the former music hall and present theatre's boards, Mother Marnes, it seems, will not perform to order, or at least not for strangers.

In 2002, a woman in grey was seen by multiple witnesses following an actor into the toilet area beneath the balcony. Fortunately perhaps for the young man, he emerged unaware of his chaperone. In 2004, an actor who was running late for a rehearsal rushed past an old lady dressed in grey sitting at the bottom of the stairs which lead to the balcony. By the time he asked the rest of the cast who she was, the woman was nowhere

The stairs which lead to the Gatehouse's haunted gallery. The ghost of Mother Marnes has been seen sitting on the chair in the corridor, and following actors into the adjacent toilet. (© Dave Milner)

bar and basement are not devoid of ghostly manifestations. During the 1980s, the eating area adjacent to the ladies' toilets was avoided by staff late at night. This area is on a slightly lower level than the bar, and extends downwards towards what was once a stable. Staff at the time were reluctant to enter this area to collect glasses after the pub closed for the night, and claim to have experienced drastic drops in temperature and glimpses of a darkly clad figure. One barmaid claimed that whilst she was cleaning tables late at night some invisible force attempted to strangle her, just as it had Tony Abbot in 1966 (although Mr Abbott's recollections were not to come to light until 1991). She promptly cancelled all her shifts, refusing to return to The Gatehouse again, and for some time after this staff refused to enter the area after hours except in pairs. Around this time the 'typical' signs that a pub may be haunted were also witnessed, such as bottles falling from shelves and smashing. Extensive remodelling in the early 1990s seems to have driven whatever was harassing the staff underground, as in recent years the focus of reported activity has been the basement.

to be found. Strangely, the chair in question is a modern plastic affair, only some twenty or so years old, and has no historical significance.

Some ten years after the last reported sighting of the lady in grey who will be forever known as Mother Marnes, her presence is still said to be felt, although she does seem to be fading. But as John Plews self-consciously remarks: 'I do see something moving out of the corner of my eye on that balcony. Quite often, actually. But it has to be my mind playing tricks. It has to be. Doesn't it?'

A Nocturnal Menace in the Restaurant

Although Mother Marnes's appearances seem to be limited to the upper levels of The Gatehouse, the main

Friendly Ghosts in the Cellar

Rather like the supernatural occurrences in the theatre upstairs, relations between the living and the departed seem to have thawed in recent years. In October 2012 Katy Wichanski, who took over the management of The Gatehouse in the spring of that year, seemed unconcerned about her spectral

Mickey and Louise Gocool of North London Paranormal Investigations demonstrate a live video feed from the haunted basement of The Gatehouse in 2012. (© Dave Milner)

houseguests, and even quite fond of them. At least two have even been given their own nicknames. 'We have two ghosts in the cellar, Francis and Stephen,' Katy claimed. 'Things sometimes fall off the shelves when they shouldn't. But they aren't nasty ghosts, quite cheeky in fact, and have been known to pinch members of staff in the cellar.'

North London Paranormal Investigations were invited to carry out an investigation in the Gatehouse's basement at Hallowe'en 2012, which was screened live in the public bar above. Using remotely controlled night-vision cameras, a spirit voice box and EMF readers, they attempted to make and capture contact with who or what was lurking in the cellar. Echoing the results of previous teams' investigations over the decades, Katy observed, 'when

we were in the cellar the orbs seemed to be following me around. It was odd because they didn't seem to be following anyone who didn't work there.'

The Flask

Sitting slightly to the north of Swains Lane, in exclusive South Grove, The Flask is today one of the most popular gastropubs in Highgate. With its glorious hanging baskets, famous Sunday lunches, and iconic red-brick frontage, The Flask is a magnet for locals as well as those wishing to imbibe some of Highgate's untouched past. It is also popular with celebrity-spotters, claiming locals Jude Law, Kate Moss and George Michael among its as regular punters. The generally held assumption

The centuries-old Flask public house in Highgate Village. (© David Farrant)

is that The Flask acquired its name from the vessels which were sold to health-seeking holidaymakers, passing through Highgate towards Hampstead's chalybeate wells. We first read of the building being referred to as an inn in 1716, although records and engravings indicate that a building existed on this site much earlier on. Steeped in history, the oldest parts of The Flask have been dated to 1663.

A reminder of The Flask's past was brought to light with the recent discovery of two gravestones in the (private) vegetable patch, indicating that the land may have been utilised as a burial space in the late 1830s, when the graveyard attached to Highgate school had reached capacity. More gruesomely, from time to time black chalkboards around the pub proclaim its cool stone hollows to have been the site of the first ever autopsy. While this claim is impossible to verify, it is certainly true that during

the nineteenth century what are now dining areas were often utilised as temporary morgues in cases of unexplained or violent death, and that autopsies were indeed carried out on the premises.

A Fleeing Cavalier

It would perhaps be incongruous for such an ancient public house not to harbour a ghost, and true to form The Flask can claim at least four. One of these, sighted as recently as the summer of 2012, is that of a cavalier in full period costume who is seen vanishing through a pillar in the upper bar, close to the site of the old cottages. The present live-in manager, Glyn Morgan, is a self-proclaimed cynic regarding all things paranormal, and relayed the sighting to this author somewhat reluctantly. The witness to this spectre was a gentleman on a short business trip, enjoying his first (and last) visit to The Flask. According to Glyn, this unfortunate stranger in town had ordered some lunch and was generally minding his own business. Tucking in, he glanced up to see the full apparition of a man garbed in doublet, cape, jerkin and decorative hat, striding towards him across the bar. As he stared, the apparition walked into a pillar between the bar and the kitchen area and did not re-emerge. After proclaiming loudly 'what the hell was that?' or less polite words to the same effect, the businessman described what he had seen. Upon being informed by the bemused bar staff that it must be the ghostly cavalier which had been known to walk the pub for so many years, the disgruntled customer stormed out, with the parting words, 'And you think this is *normal?*'

The concept of the shade of a cavalier manifesting in an 'olde worlde' pub may seem twee in the first analysis. However, visibly distinguishing oneself as a cavalier or a roundhead would have been an almost tribal mark of identity for anyone moneyed living in seventeenth-century Highgate. The English Civil War of 1642 to 1651, and the years on either side of it, had an extremely divisive effect upon prominent families who owned land in the village. The fear of having one's home seized or, worse, being arrested and executed for treason would have been constant. That the area which this cavalier appears to be moving towards would have originally been an outbuilding, with no public access, could suggest that he was attempting to escape into a place of safety, from pursuers of some kind. One legend associated

The snug bar of The Flask public house as it appeared in 2005, prior to remodelling. To the right can be seen the Old Monk's Bench, now removed. To the left the legendary bullet hole is circled, and in the distance can be seen the pillar through which the ghost of a cavalier was seen disappearing as recently as 2012. (© Alys Tomlinson)

with The Flask tells of a bullet lodged in a wall of the snug bar. When I asked Glyn to show me the famous bullet, he sighed and informed me that it was actually just a small hole in the wall. I sighed too upon discovering that the wall has recently been covered with an artificial sheet of carefully aged ply, and the bullet hole is no longer visible. In Glyn's opinion the hole, whatever its origin, was created during the 1930s as this is when the now covered pitch panelling was installed. This earlier decoration corresponds with English Heritage's 1974 survey of The Flask, the bullet – if it ever existed – having been removed long ago by a gleeful tourist. Those of a romantic disposition may still be intrigued by the observation of this author that the exact placement of the mystery bullet corresponds with the trajectory of someone entering the snug, and firing in the direction of the vanishing cavalier, missing their moving target by some 6 inches

Secret Tunnels and Chambers

Any secret room or tunnel which is rumoured to exist in the village's antiquated houses, or under its narrow streets, instantly generates fresh myths about Dick Turpin and his many alleged getaway routes. As political strife throughout the seventeenth century turned Catholic against Protestant, and divided families, neighbours and friends, the need to protect oneself at short notice clearly suggests a more plausible reason for these occulted chambers. One such den exists under The Flask itself, and hints deliciously at secrets which were so well kept that they died with those who guarded them.

In November 1899, members of the Highgate Harriers running club were ambling home after practice when they noticed that one of their members, Thomas Blake, was missing. Upon retracing their steps they discovered a subsidence in the road, whereupon:

> It was discovered that Blake had disappeared into the cavity, which was about six feet wide and fifteen feet deep. An examination of the cavity led to the discovery that the upper portion of a subterranean passage had collapsed, and on tracing the course of this passage another was discovered. The main tunnel, which is of considerable circumference, leads to the left to The Flask Tavern in South-grove, opposite St Michael's church, and on the right it is said to lead to Ken Wood.
> (*Evening Standard*, 3 November 1899)

The supposition that the tunnel into which the boy fell really does lead to (or from) The Flask has remained the stuff of local legend – until now. A former chief architect for Benskins brewery contacted this author with some remarkable information about a discovery made during 1974 renovations to The Flask:

> My men were working under a small single-storey addition in the corner of the forecourt on the right-hand side, which at that time was in use as a bottle store. One workman was using a pickaxe to cut out a pit for a sump, and it went straight through and knocked out a hole, which they widened. They found a tunnel, half full of soft sand but big enough overall for someone to crawl through, under the cellar floor. The tunnel was circular,

brick-lined and roughly 1.5m in diameter. Littered here and there were some old clay pipes, and they got the overall impression that it had been used as a hideout many centuries back. There was a policy of 'no antiquities on this site', something which is very common on building sites I can tell you, and a lot of things go unrecorded. The hole was made good with the minimum of fuss!

Could this secret chamber explain the presence of the fleeing cavalier? Allan Fea's *Secret Chambers and Hiding Places* (1901) informs us that the Highgate home of Ireton, Cromwell's son-in-law was equipped with 'a large secret chamber at the back of a cupboard in one of the upper rooms, and extended back twelve or fourteen feet'. With numerous other tunnels alleged to exist around the village, including one which leads from the site of Andrew Marvell's cottage on North Hill to Cromwell House, a rather Monty Python-esque picture begins to form of one half of Highgate interchangeably hiding from the other throughout the entirety of the 1600s.

A Jacobean Ghost on The Old Monk's Bench

For many years a wooden bench stood against the wall of The Flask's snug, facing the bar. That this heavily carved pew-style seat was a genuine seventeenth-century piece indicates that it may well have been a survivor from The Flask's early days as a manorial court, when the accused would have sat in the snug awaiting their hearings. Sadly the bench was removed some years ago to make way for more modern seating. For decades prior to this, however, regulars took the occasional manifestation of

a shadowy form sitting on the bench as a given, to the extent that it became known as 'The Old Monk's Bench'. The most detailed sighting comes from a Mr Tim Roberts of Muswell Hill. In spring 1976, at around seven in the evening, Tim was enjoying a drink with a friend in the snug. After his friend stepped outside briefly, Tim became aware of a movement to his right. Glancing over, Tim recalls clearly seeing what appeared to be a tall man in late 1600s garb ('a Quaker-type figure', to quote Tim precisely), leaning forward with his hands clasped around a cane. With no table to block his view, Tim was able to note the mysterious man's black trousers and full waistcoat, white frilled shirt and black bowl-topped hat. His attention briefly distracted, Tim looked back to find that the vision had vanished. He could still recall vividly the man's pale face and thin grey hair, which flowed down over his ears.

Old May's Lost Cottage

Another ghost to make its presence felt strongly during the 1970s was that of 'Old May', a former inhabitant of the cottages to the left of the pub. According to Highgate 'old-timer' Les Chapman, who is very proud of his knowledge of the to-ings and fro-ings of local spooks, Old May had been hanging around The Flask for years, but began haunting her previous home with a vengeance in the mid-1970s. Staff living on site began hearing the sound of furniture being moved around and an indistinct fumbling sound which would keep them awake for hours, while one particular door would open and close by itself, despite being carefully locked.

The aforementioned architect from Benskins brewery recalled that, during the same period as the tunnel discovery, his team converted the old cottages into accommodation for the staff, a role they still play. If substantial renovations to property really can reawaken dormant psychic energy, this could lend weight to Les's story. It could also account for the decline in manifestations by 'Old May' as the changes to the structure of the historic Flask became embedded and settled down. Despite this comforting conclusion, even arch-sceptic Glyn Morgan in an interview for the *Ham & High* in January 2013 conceded, when asked if he had ever seen anything in The Flask: 'No, I haven't, but we have had quite a few doors lock themselves, and strange things like that.'

Within the exhaustive records pertaining to The Flask's many owners, the only potential 'May' to be found who spent any length of time at The Flask is a Mary Hooper. Hooper is described as a spinster from London, and she acquired the tavern in 1692, so may well have known William Blake, who in Chapter 2 is suggested as a possible suspect for the figure on the Old Monk's Bench. It is almost amusing to visualise the re-energised ghost of Old May clinging on to her cottage for dear life, aware that 'Madman Blake' was also lurking 20 or so yards away, perhaps still hankering after her land. If ghosts hold conversations we remain unprivy to them, but were this possible the exchanges between these two seventeenth-century relics would certainly be worth an eavesdrop.

If Old May had accepted the new-look Flask by the 1980s, some other energy was certainly at work in 1987

and 1988, around the same time that The Gatehouse found itself suddenly compromised once again by what seemed to be supernatural phenomena. Approaching Christmas time 1987, Ginger McGarry, the then general manager of The Flask, was witness to what seemed to be some startling poltergeist activity. In an interview the following year, he described a holly wreath hanging in the snug being 'hurled' some 8 feet across the room and landing in the middle of the floor. Two weeks later both of the pub's clocks, which were maintained on separate electrical circuits, stopped at precisely 5.20 p.m. – the pub's then opening time. On 11 January a bottle of lager flew from a shelf and smashed violently on the floor of the snug, as two light bulbs simultaneously blew, also shattering glass about the bar.

A Tragic Spanish Barmaid

The spectral cavalier is not the only ghost at The Flask who has put customers off their food in more recent years. In *Haunted London* (2007) Richard Jones refers to an incident a few years previously when a female clairvoyant and three friends were visiting The Flask for lunch. Suddenly they declared that they were leaving, the clairvoyant rapidly explaining that 'while the aura of the ghost was friendly, its presence was overwhelming, and she found it quite disturbing. "That ghost cost me four lunches," lamented Andy the manager.'

Jones suggests that the ghost encountered by the clairvoyant was The Flask's most famous supernatural resident, that of a Spanish barmaid who is alleged to have hanged herself in one of the several underground level ante-chambers in use as seating areas today. Unfortunately, the origins of this tragic figure's tale have been lost to time, but traditionally she is held to have killed herself after her employer rejected her amorous advances. The popular Spaniards Inn, constructed in 1585 in nearby Hampstead, has been suggested to be the summer retreat of 1600s Spanish ambassador Count Gondemar. This link could explain the nameless barmaid's passage to England, as could a former landlord of The Spaniards, Francis Porrero, who has been mooted as the inspiration for the pub's name. Sightings of this female ghost have so far proven impossible to track down, but allegedly she makes her presence felt by swift drops in temperature, and gentle cool breezes down the back of customers' necks.

Fabrice, a cleaner, and his wife, who have spent many hours alone in The Flask in the early hours of the morning, have had some very unnerving experiences in the oldest parts of the pub. These were at their worst in the summers of 2012 and 2013, when on balmy nights the temperature would suddenly drop to that of a refrigerator. The couple also recall that the hairs on their arms would rise, along with the unmistakable sense of someone standing close behind them, watching their every move. The ghost seems to have been particularly interested in Fabrice, whom it would follow from room to room, leaving its footprints on the freshly mopped floors, and its finger marks on newly polished surfaces. Perhaps he bears some resemblance to her lost love?

5

HAUNTED HOUSES

By now it may strike the reader that much of Highgate's paranormal activity appears to take place outdoors, or in public houses. But it seems that there is equally little comfort to be found in some of its private residences.

The House that Dripped Blood

Of the many volunteers who have contributed their time and energy to restoring and conserving Highgate Cemetery, Jean Pateman (1921–2012) is without doubt the best known. Born in Cheshire, Mrs Pateman moved to Highgate in 1958 with her husband John and their three young children, after a five-year residency in Hampstead. This followed a stint in South Africa, which was terminated by her husband's forced resignation as headmaster of the exclusive Hilton College, Natal, after several disputes about his teaching methods. John Pateman's perceived fall from grace affected their social status in England greatly. According to the unofficial

obituary *Mrs Tombstone – A Life*, penned by former Highgate Cemetery volunteer Caroline Coombes, Mrs Pateman was 'bitterly aware' of the difficulties she faced while attempting her *entré* into the insular world of Highgate high society. Mrs Pateman went on to carve a unique niche for herself, and eventually achieved a position of influence and authority. Her reputation for dismissing all references to the cemetery's supernatural traditions outlives her, particularly her horror of the mention of 'vampires'. But what is generally unknown is that the house in Highgate which Mrs Pateman occupied for fifty-four years was reputedly heavily haunted …

Situated slightly to the north-west of Highgate Village, 5 View Road, built around 1914, as of 2014 stands empty and under consideration for demolition. But this attractive, twenty-roomed mansion made international headlines on 21 December 1955 when in a report circulated by Reuters, its then occupant Mrs Doris Hatton-Wood claimed that the house had been invaded by 'black magic spirits', and 'devilish forces so strong' that 'even two priests could not exorcise them'.

> 'There were mysterious bloodstains on the wall,' the widow's housekeeper Mrs Winifred Allsop said firmly: 'We didn't imagine it, I saw them myself. They were running down the duck-egg blue walls.' And a large oil painting mysteriously 'hurled itself' at Mrs Hatton-Wood as she passed it on the stairs. 'That painting was secured by two chains,' she said.

Other manifestations of something 'diabolical' occurred: the two women were regularly disturbed by 'strange footsteps, weird bangings which seemed to come from between the walls, sounds of heavy boxes being dragged across the floors, an apparition of a dog, and glassware and crockery being broken'. When the situation became unbearable, Mrs Hatton-Wood wrote to the Reverend Gilbert Shaw, 'a priest active in combating black magic'. Duly, Fr Shaw:

in black cassock and accompanied by the Father Superior of a monastery, paid a visit to the old mansion. They sprinkled holy water over the rooms and the grounds of the house. 'Things are a bit better now,' said Mrs Hatton-Wood, 'but we still hear the strange sounds. I intend to write to the priests again. I hope they will come back.'

Whether or not Fr Shaw (1886–1967) returned to perform a full exorcism is unrecorded, but conversations between this author and close friends of this well-respected priest and authorised exorcist affirmed Shaw's sincerity, and dedication to his pastoral duties. To point out that this somewhat violent haunting would have been an embarrassment for Jean Pateman, with her verbose condemnation of all things paranormal, is belabouring the obvious. Subsequently, whether Mrs Pateman experienced similar phenomena during her half-century occupancy of 5 View Road remains a secret which she took with her to the grave.

A Golf Course with a Sinister Secret

So why was this detached villa infested by what were described as 'black magic spirits'? A possible answer may be found in a *cause célèbre* which shook the nation, and occurred just a quarter of a mile away to the west, at what is now Highgate Golf Club. Twenty-five feet beneath the twelfth hole lie buried the foundations of what was once a grand hunting lodge, referred to in the fourteenth century as the 'Bishop's Palace'.

Surrounded by a moat, this 70 square feet motte and bailey style building was used as accommodation for hunting parties and other privileged guests of successive bishops of London within whose vast lands it once sat, a privilege conferred by their roles as lords of the manor of Hornsey. It was here in 1441 that a black mass – or a series of such masses – allegedly took place, which, had they been successful, would have altered the course of British history.

Born Eleanor Cobham, in around 1400, the Duchess of Gloucester was known as an ambitious social climber. Like many nobles of her time, she studied astrology, under the guidance of her personal astrologer Roger Bolingbroke. She also engaged the services of a 'witch', Margery Jourdemayne, known as the 'Witch of Eye', who supposedly provided her with fertility charms. In July 1441, Eleanor, Jourdemayne, Bolingbroke, Thomas Southwell (the canon of St Stephen's, Westminster) and John Hume (the canon of Hereford), were accused of heretical sorcery. Their alleged intention was to end the life of the 'boy king' Henry VI, thus enabling his brother, Humphrey, Duke of Gloucester, to accede to the throne. This would by default make Henry's aunt, Eleanor, Queen of England. With the privacy afforded by the remote and fortified lodge at Highgate, the group were charged with melting wax effigies of the king before the fire, that they might 'consume the King's person by way of negromancie and [saying] masses in the Lodge of Hornsey Park near London, upon certaine instruments with which the said Sir Roger should use his craft of negromancie, against the faith'.

Harsh sentences were handed down to all but Hume, who was pardoned. Jourdemayne was burned at the stake at Smithfields, while Bolingbroke was hanged, drawn and quartered. Southwell died in prison, possibly by his own hand, before his turn to mount the scaffold came. Eleanor was sentenced to public atonement, and made to walk the streets of London barefoot and bareheaded, carrying a lit taper for three consecutive nights. She was forced to divorce her husband and stripped of all ranks and titles, before being imprisoned for life. Among the various strongholds in which she was incarcerated were Leeds Castle, and Peel Castle on the Isle of Man. Interestingly, both boast legends of ghostly black dogs, or 'shucks', which claim links to Eleanor's imprisonment. For many centuries a tavern stood in Highgate by the name of The Black Dog, which may or may not be a coincidence.

The lodge's sinister reputation probably contributed to its neglect, and by 1593, when surveyed by Norden, little remained, save for:

> two deep ditches, now old and overgrown with bushes; the rubble thereof, as brick, tile, and Cornish slate, are in heaps yet to be seen, which ruins are of great antiquity, as may appear by the oaks at this day standing, above a hundred years growth, upon the very foundation of the building.

The moat was still evident by 1843, when it was used 'as a watering place for cattle; the aged bushes on its banks [may yet be seen] drooping into the refreshing stream', and its ditch is still clearly visible in modern aerial photographs.

Could the negative energy invoked during these rituals still be active, and could it have played a part in the chaotic disturbances at 5 View Road? If there is any validity in the often-asserted claim that water acts as an amplifier for psychic forces, perhaps the construction of a reservoir with a 40 million litre capacity by the Metropolitan Water Board in 1928, between the tenth and thirteenth holes, is significant.

A Haunted Council Estate

Until recent years, with the exception of a handful of famous cases such as the Enfield poltergeist, and the black monk of Pontefract, modern council houses were not typically associated with paranormal phenomena. Perhaps this is because they do not inspire active imaginations with the same degree of fluidity that the eerie atmospheres of ancient castles and stately homes can lend. The elegantly landscaped Hillcrest Estate, which sits on a hulking prominence of land just above Highgate Village known as the Bulwarks, certainly does not present an ominous prospect to the uninitiated. But for generations, stories have circulated among residents of this post-war estate with its innovative design and lofty trees, of a shadowy figure haunting the grounds and various flats. At one stage in 1979 at least fifteen occupants of the seven eight-storey blocks of flats which occupy this 5-acre site could claim to have witnessed or encountered the figure.

Park House, on the site now occupied by Hillcrest. At this time it was in use as an 'Asylum for Idiots'. (Author's collection)

Perhaps then it is no surprise that the land upon which Hillcrest is situated has a long history of habitation, much of it troubled. In days gone by it was occupied by Park House, a mansion used between 1848 and 1855 as an asylum, and from then until 1940 as the mercilessly cruel 'House of Mercy' penitentiary for 'fallen' women. In this militant establishment, which had much in common with Ireland's Magdalene laundries, young women, who had often been forced into prostitution, were forcibly separated from their illegitimate offspring and spent (in some cases) decades confined to a life of hard labour.

Identified from war records as the possible site of a Napoleonic hill fort, a network of brick-lined tunnels was discovered in 1982 dug deep into the hillside, the origin of which has never

been fully established. The Hillcrest Estate itself has had more than its fair share of misery over the years, with a disproportionate number of suicides and tragedies afflicting the families who have made it their home.

Betty and John Goodchild moved into Alexander House at Hillcrest with their three children in 1970, and quickly sensed that they were not alone in their new home. Betty was the first to experience an uncanny feeling of being watched, whilst reading late at night in the living room. Soon she began to notice a fleeting figure pass the door, and retreat down the hallway, something which every member of her family would eventually experience. John was next to notice their unwanted houseguest, when he began being awoken by 'a low whispering sound

Tunnels discovered under Hillcrest in 1982. (© Hornsey Historical Society)

echoing around the flat'. This was always eventually traced to the front room, where it would cease abruptly upon John's 'intrusion'. Soon afterwards both he and Betty began experiencing the distinct sensation of someone sitting down on their bed at night. At first the couple kept their concerns from the children so as not to worry them. By the late 1970s, however, all three children had echoed their parents' belief that an invisible stranger was present in the flat. Many families on the estate had also had tales relayed to them by their children of a tall, greyish form seen in daylight moving across the grass and vanishing into the block adjacent to Alexander House.

By 1979 the Goodchilds' youngest son Robert was unable to sleep alone in his bedroom, after persistent waking nightmares about 'something horrible' entering his room made sleep impossible for the whole family. Aside from Robert's nocturnal screaming, another noise which his older sister Jan remembered frequently hearing was the sound of breathing from the living room.

One of the most disturbing sounds, which the whole family were party to thrice, was the heart-wrenching crying of a baby. This would begin at a high pitch in the early hours of the morning and then decrease in volume, quite unlike the sound of a living baby being picked up and comforted by its mother. Each of

Alexander House at Hillcrest, where at least three residents reported nocturnal disturbances. (© Della Farrant)

Other manifestations of something untoward continued to plague the Goodchilds. A recently framed photograph was wrenched from an undamaged nail and smashed on the floor, tearing its brass chain in half. An electronic doorbell began to chime repeatedly at 2 a.m., even after an exhausted John Goodchild began removing the batteries nightly. As the years went by, Jan moved out to raise her own family, and it quickly became noticeable that, when visiting Alexander House, her baby daughter would become transfixed by something moving about in the front room just below the ceiling. In desperation, John and Betty finally decided to request the services of their local vicar, in an attempt to cleanse their home of its unwanted presence. If anything, this seemed to make things worse, and not just for the Goodchilds.

A chance conversation about their children's sightings of 'something weird' gliding about on the grounds of the estate led to an extraordinary and long-overdue exchange of experiences between the Goodchilds and two of their neighbours. All three households were relieved and disturbed in equal measures upon discovering that whatever the entity plaguing the Goodchilds was, it had been manifesting in the two adjacent flats, and in a similar fashion.

Roger Clarke, in his 2012 work *A Natural History of Ghosts*, proposes the idea that periods of economic downturn can exacerbate incidents of 'poltergeist' phenomena. Perhaps it is relevant then, that the majority of disturbances reported on the Hillcrest Estate can be dated to one of the most uncertain and distressing periods in Britain's economic history. This era encompassed, for example, the famous 'three-day working week' measures introduced by the Tory government in 1974 to

these occasions heralded the unnatural demise of a resident of the estate. The fear which this generated in the family was paralleled on a subsequent occasion, when Jan and Robert both burst into the front room around midnight, protesting that something invisible had woken them up and turned their rooms icy cold. As they relayed their terror, the family's pet cat Elsa began to hiss and spit at something in the corner of the room, which had itself dropped dramatically in temperature. Concluding the obvious – that the entity had followed the children into the living room – the family sat up all night together until daybreak.

conserve electricity. As residents from this time recall, mass unemployment and the recessions of the early 1970s and 1980s also contributed to low morale, which along with cramped conditions could certainly have lit the touch paper that enabled so much negative psychical activity to explode.

Some seventeen years later, it was a cold, unfurnished top-floor flat in Wavell House which Deborah Meredith (see Chapter 1) found herself relocated to by Haringey Council on, of all days, Hallowe'en, 1996. While the first six months or so of her tenancy at Hillcrest were uncomfortable and slightly unnerving, the subsequent two and a half years were the stuff of nightmares.

Working until 6 a.m. as a taxi driver, Deborah would park her cab in the deserted bay some 20 yards from her block and hurry back as quickly as she could. At first she attributed the recurrent and indistinct figure, which seemed to follow at a short distance behind her, to shadows cast by the many trees that rise up the bank upon which Hillcrest rests. However, the climb up the hundreds of steps to her flat soon became something to dread, when she noticed that the connecting doors on the landings which closed behind her were regularly being opened and closed again by someone else ascending the stairwell. No one was ever visible through the spyhole when she gained the 'safety' of her flat, but the sense of being watched did not diminish. On some occasions Deborah would catch sight of an extraordinarily tall, dark figure on the eighth-floor balcony, seemingly staring in through the net curtain. Things soon got worse, and Deborah found herself seeking medical advice when she began being woken repeatedly in the night with feelings of paralysis, accompanied by heart palpitations and the

A building on the Hillcrest Estate, much like the one where Deborah Meredith recalls being followed up the stairs to her fifth-floor flat by an invisible agency. (© Della Farrant)

sensation of someone sucking the breath out of her lungs. These attacks would cause her to run to the bathroom for reviving cold water, and contributed to her growing feelings of anxiety, especially after her GP gave her a clean bill of health.

Events culminated one night in the summer of 1999, when, after experiencing a sudden drop in temperature, Deborah was terrified by an ear-splitting bang and a smashing sound from the front-room window. After leaping from her chair expecting to be covered with glass, she discovered no damage, but witnessed a large comet-like flash of light passing through the window and into her flat with 'an intense force'. She watched, petrified, as it dropped towards the floor and, moving into the hall through the wall, disappeared from sight. Upon steeling herself up, and searching the flat, Deborah could find no trace of the mysterious football-sized sphere of light. Whether what Deborah saw that night can be explained by the phenomena of ball lightning can never

be known. If the glowing shape *was* ball lightning, as some readers may naturally speculate, no obvious natural causation for its generation, or reason for its attraction to this eighth-floor flat, is apparent. Whatever its explanation, this experience contributed towards Deborah's conclusion just days later that she had no choice but to leave Hillcrest for good.

A Wailing Ghost in Holly Village

A remnant of the Holly Lodge Estate, Holly Village, which was developed in 1865 by Baroness Burdett-Coutts for her vast staff, is today one of Britain's most exclusive residences. This gated enclave, which consists of twelve houses designed in an elaborate high gothick style, has attracted many famous occupants over the years. One of these, singer Lynsey De Paul, experienced a variety of strange goings-on during the 1970s shortly after moving into

Holly Village, the gothick home of singer Lynsey de Paul. (© Dave Milner)

this unique community. In various interviews Ms De Paul recollected some fairly intense poltergeist activity. Some of these incidents were alarming, such as electrical cables bursting into flame, doors opening and closing unaided, and heavy mirrors and stained-glass windows smashing spontaneously. Others had a more mischievous aspect, such as the occasion when, having searched the entire house for her missing door keys, Ms De Paul eventually found them hidden in the freezer

In 2008 the late Ingrid Pitt, star of so many Hammer Horror films, recalled a recent conversation with Ms De Paul, in which she jubilantly declared that after three decades of living with a ghost, her home was now spook-free. Having been plagued for years by the piteous sobbing of a young child, Ms De Paul had eventually devised a novel means by which to 'exorcise' the spirit. 'Nothing was known of the child,' remembered Ingrid:

> or how it became unhappy but Lynsey was determined to do something about it. What do you do to soothe a crying child? Read it *Alice in Wonderland*, of course! Personally I have never been a big fan of the smarmy Alice. I've always hoped to see a version where the Queen of Hearts goes through with her threat to separate her pinny from her Alice Band. But it seems that the Wailing Waif didn't have the same problem. Lynsey's house is now waifless.

The Police are Perplexed by a Poltergeist

Heading back to the village, at the junction of Highgate Hill and the High Street we find 'Fairseat', now the Channing School. Rebuilt in 1867 by Sir Sydney Waterlow, its last occupant, this imposing Victorian mansion replaced a much earlier building which can be dated back to the 1600s. Harry Price notes in *Poltergeist over England: Three Centuries of Mischievous Ghosts* (1945) that during December 1942 Fairseat was in the process of being converted into a 'British Restaurant'. These government-run establishments existed to ensure that bombed-out or otherwise impoverished Britons had daily access to at least one cooked meal. During renovations to Fairseat, according to two contemporary newspaper reports of 21 December 1942 archived by Price:

> workmen complained that their tools were being moved to distant parts of the house, bells were rung, materials disappeared, and 'the most weird noises are heard'. A policeman heard a bell ringing in the middle of the night. He had the house surrounded, and investigated, but the bell-ringer was never discovered.

Ritual Remains Discovered in Lauderdale House

Adjacent to Fairseat stands Lauderdale House, a beautifully restored stately home built in 1582. Situated within Waterlow Park and steeped in history, Lauderdale House has an almost suspicious lack of recorded ghost activity. This could be due to the secretion behind a chimney breast in the mid-1600s of an astonishing hoard of ritual objects. Discovered resting inside a wicker basket during renovations carried out in the early 1960s, the gruesome artefacts seem to be the gathered remnants of a magical ceremony, in all

Some of the gruesome ritual remains discovered in the chimney breast at Lauderdale House in 1962. (© Dr Chris Laoutaris)

probability designed to protect the house and its occupants from negative influences. They include four chickens (two strangled and two walled up alive), an egg, two shoes, a candlestick, a chalice and a plaited rush, which is suggestive of some form of knot magic. Whatever ceremony was conducted in the house all those centuries ago seems to have been effective, for despite a terrible fire which broke out in 1963 shortly after the removal of the objects, the house still stands proud, and apparently un-haunted, today.

A Haunted Scout Hut

Slightly to the south of Lauderdale House stands St Joseph's church, built in 1875–76. During the 1950s and 1960s a scouts' den existed in the grounds of 'Holy Joe's', as it is known locally, which was approached along a dirt track and held many tales for the brave boys who made it to the hut. These all revolved around a Mrs Speary, an unfortunate lady who died on the land many years

back after slipping on the snow there. An elderly woman in old-fashioned clothes has been seen many times by adults as well as children, at least as far back as the 1930s, walking up the track and then just disappearing.

A Racketing Ghost in Elthorne Road

An interesting echo of the disturbances at Hillcrest is found the following account, which appears in Sharon Jones's *Dead Zones* (1992):

> At the bottom of Highgate Hill, on Elthorne Road, is an apartment that was besieged with poltergeist activity in 1978. A vague outline of a figure was seen on the walls, and heavy objects were moved about by an unseen hand. Family members and neighbours experienced a series of bizarre activities and finally resorted to holding a cleansing and blessing ceremony. The ghostly festivities ceased after that.

The area around Elthorne Road had a sinister reputation in centuries past, being bordered by what was previously known as 'Devil's Lane', named for the moated and desolate 'Devil's House' which once stood nearby.

A Playful Ghost at Cloisters Court

Crossing Highgate Hill, at the beginning of Cromwell Avenue, one reaches Cloisters Court, formerly the Highgate United Reformed church but since converted into flats. Mrs Kate Marks lived in one of these flats between 1983 and 1986, and one night was startled from her sleep. Sensing that she was not alone, Kate propped herself up and squinted towards the end of the room, which was illuminated by the light from the hallway. Suddenly she was aware of a movement to her left, and a young boy, rather like Peter Pan with his missing shadow, dashed across the room and through the wall. Unnerved for several months, Kate made enquiries and managed to ascertain that her flat was the part of the church previously used for holding Sunday school. Once she felt assured that the child was merely playing, and not running in fear, Kate ceased to be frightened by what she today refers to as 'my little ghost'.

Cloisters Court, the former Highgate United Reformed church, now converted into flats. (© Dave Milner)

An Unsuccessful Exorcism in Cromwell Avenue

Continuing up Cromwell Avenue, we encounter two more hauntings, of a less light-hearted nature. Cromwell Avenue, which runs northeast from Highgate Village towards Archway Road, was developed in the early 1880s, upon land once belonging to the Winchester Hall estate. It is this mansion from which The Winchester public house on Archway Road takes its name, and not, as suggested by zombie-hunting Ed in the 2004 cult movie *Shaun of the Dead*, from a Winchester rifle hanging above the bar. The earliest reference to Winchester Hall appears in 1603, and it was rebuilt several times before its demolition in 1881. Examination of the parish plan of 1864 shows that Cromwell Avenue was built along one of the oldest paths within the estate, which may itself have utilised an earlier track way.

Nicholas Palma, previously quoted in Chapter 1, grew up in Highgate Village and has many happy memories of his boyhood there during the 1980s. But one prolonged episode mars these for Nick.

In 1986 his family home was found to have major structural concerns, necessitating a temporary move into another property while repairs were carried out. At short notice Nick's parents were delighted to sign a six-month lease on an empty Victorian house, at the Highgate Hill end of much coveted Cromwell Avenue. From the day they moved into the street Nick, then aged 13 or 14, found the atmosphere brooding, and as he puts it, 'saturated with some dark menace'. His sense of foreboding proved to be accurate, as before the family had even finished unpacking they became acutely aware that something about the house 'just wasn't right'.

Doors slammed of their own accord. Electrical equipment, especially the television set, began to function erratically, and every member of the family – who had always been close – sensed the oppressive and negative presence of an 'invisible being' in their midst. With the heightened observational skills that we perhaps all have as children, Nick became convinced that whatever was sharing the house with them was rapidly, and with some ease, driving a palpable wedge between his usually loving parents. Suggestive of scenes from the book and motion picture *The Amityville Horror*, relationships within the family began to quickly break down, as blazing and pointless arguments suddenly replaced cosy family nights in. To compound the oddness of the entire situation, the family noticed strange, high-pitched whining noises, and after some consternation discovered that the sounds originated from several neighbourhood cats, which were congregating almost nightly outside the house and crying in distress.

Soon events took an even more frightening turn. In the midst of the familial discord, Nick claims that he began to be visited by a darkly clad figure as he lay in bed at night. Increasingly terrified by these nightly invasions, Nick could only lie frozen with fear as the entity, which he describes as male and of broad and tall proportions, stood motionlessly observing him. As Nick recalls: 'My parents even brought a priest round to perform a blessing, in the hope that this would banish whatever haunted the house. It didn't work.'

Unable to cope with the stifling atmosphere in the house, and concerned for Nick's safety, the Palmas moved back to their own home sooner than planned. Later research into the previous occupants of the residence (it would be insensitive to specify the street number in print) reveals that the family who rented the house before the Palmas had also felt forced to vacate the premises. Some of these family members are also reported to have received acute psychiatric intervention as a result of their experiences, although I have been unable to verify this. According to Nick, who traced friends of the family at the time, they had tried in some way to make contact with the 'spirits' who occupied the house, and these attempts had dramatically exacerbated the negative atmosphere which pervaded the house. As I did not wish to alarm the current residents whilst researching this haunting, I cannot confirm whether these manifestations are still active today.

Saved from Death by a Ghost?

Brian Sutcliffe also spent his childhood in Highgate, and during his teenage years lived in Cromwell Avenue. Although this was during the late 1960s and early 1970s, the Victorian house still had a row of servants' bells, which although long since disconnected would frequently send a peal of startling sounds through the ground-floor flat which Brian and his parents occupied. The smell of cooking would also waft between the rooms, when no meal had been prepared, and on at least one occasion Brian's mother was awoken at 4 a.m. by a loud pounding on her bedroom door by invisible fists.

The flat had a cellar, and Brian would often chop wood for the fire at the bottom of the slatted stairs. He recalls

regularly experiencing the overwhelming sensation of someone, or 'something', watching him from the dark space under the stairs at the back of the basement. Perhaps not wishing to frighten him, Brian's mother did not share with him her identical experiences in the cellar, until he mentioned his own to her several decades later. His mother also recalled dramatic drops in temperature when the invisible voyeur manifested, and remembered feeling extremely uncomfortable should she have cause to enter the basement alone.

In the early 1970s Brian and three friends set off for Highgate Cemetery, with the intention of making a movie. He recalls that it was, unsurprisingly for the time and place:

a gory vampire sort of thing with tomato sauce blood and other easily obtainable props. We made the big gates leading to the vaults open on their own, by tying thin fishing line to the gate bottom, and having a hidden friend pull it open slowly from the bushes. The plot was not that strong.

Filming in the old cemetery completed, the BAFTA hopefuls headed for The Old Crown public house on Highgate Hill, and it was not until after midnight that Brian wended his way home to Cromwell Avenue, soaked to the skin after being caught in a bout of unanticipated torrential rain. After sneaking up to his bedroom to avoid chastisement, Brian crawled straight into bed, still wet through and fully clothed. He shut his eyes and expected to fall asleep right away, but suddenly sensed something near him. 'On opening my eyes,' Brian recalls:

I saw a priest-like form with a black hat on his head. I said 'go away' – in less polite terms! I then went to sleep. However, in the early morning I re-awoke with a stabbing pain in my back every time I breathed, which turned out to be pleurisy pneumonia; I was hospitalised for two weeks.

Some thirty years later I took my daughter up to London to show her my old haunts. We went back to the house where I used to live and knocked on the door. The lady of the house (most trustworthy) let us in after I explained to her that I used to live there. Over a coffee and ciga-rette I took a chance and told her of my experience many years back. She became very pensive and then said that her daughter had seen a form with a black hat on its head standing on the landing which frightened her – but on looking again it had gone. I was stunned, as was my daughter. The new owner also intimated that the atmos-phere was sometimes strange.

I have often felt that the entity which I saw may not have been malev-olent, but might have been warning me to change out of my wet clothes.

A Brooding Spectre on Suicide Bridge

Yamako King was born in Hampstead, and retains some disturbing childhood memories of driving across Archway Bridge, locally referred to as 'Suicide Bridge', with her mother in the mid-2000s. On the first occasion Yamako remembers seeing a shadowy figure standing on the bridge, facing south, gazing down at the road. Intrigued, she kept her gaze focused upon him, and was understandably unsettled when he simply 'disappeared whilst still in plain sight' as their car passed him. On the second occa-sion Yamako's mother suddenly jolted and screamed, just as they drove off the bridge heading west towards Highgate. She shouted, 'Did you just see that creepy faced man?' and subsequently refused to discuss what she had seen, or even to glance up at the bridge whilst driving up Archway Road. But as Yamako remem-bers, 'I could see that she looked terrified.'

The Hornsey Lane Poltergeist

I am grateful to Alan Murdie LL.B., the chair of the Society for Psychical Research's Spontaneous Cases Committee, for retrieving a brief mention in *Light* magazine from November 1928 of the 'Hornsey Lane Poltergeist' case of 1894–95. The house in question, at the junction of Hornsey Lane (which now crosses Archway Bridge) and Archway Road, was plagued for two years by the ringing of disused servants' bells, long after the cords had been cut. Like the two previously men-tioned cases wherein bells were reported to ring without the assistance of any human agency, this case was never solved. It is interesting to note, however, that the disturbances – which had never previ-ously been reported – only occurred during the demolition and subsequent rebuilding of 'Suicide Bridge'.

The Ghost who Jumped out the Window

In the winter of 1968, Jimmy Kelly, from County Roscommon in the west of Ireland, was visiting his sister Bernadette at Highgate. Bernadette at this time occupied the two upper storeys of a Victorian townhouse situated in Hornsey Lane Gardens. For the two years she had been living alone in the maisonette, Bernadette had been complaining in letters to her brother that she was worried that the house might be haunted. She had been so frightened by strange noises, and an intimidating male presence, that for the previous two summers she had even taken advantage of any warm nights by sleeping outside on the balcony.

Jimmy, who remained cynical about the 'ghost', was soon to encounter it first-hand. As the siblings sat at the kitchen table, at around 6 p.m. one evening, they both distinctly heard two loud raps on the heavy oak door. 'There it is again!' Bernadette whispered, and remained in the kitchen as Jimmy flung open the door to confront the intruder. Although he could see no one, Jimmy heard the unmistakable sound of heavy footfalls on the stairs, landing on the left, and then the right, as they ascended to the top floor. Baffled, but unlike Bernadette who was still hiding in the kitchen, unafraid, Jimmy raced up the stairs. Upon reaching the landing, he saw that the door to the spare bedroom was opening and closing by itself, and entering the room was amazed to find that, as he puts it, 'your man was nowhere to be seen'. The room was freezing cold, which Jimmy concluded must be down to the wide-open sash window, from which the invisible intruder had made his escape.

If the ghost was scared away by Jimmy's presence, it returned with a vengeance after he went home to Ireland. After waking in the night to find clammy hands squeezing her throat, Bernadette moved in with friends, and sold the haunted maisonette shortly afterwards.

The 'House of Dracula' on Avenue Road

Heading east up Hornsey Lane, on the corner of Avenue and Crescent Roads stand the remains of a neo-gothic mansion erected in 1876. Today the architraves of the original house's frontage embrace a modern housing development built on the site, but before being gutted by fire in 1969, Number 1 Avenue Road was known locally as the 'House of Dracula'. This reputation became cemented around 1973, when the unoccupied house was in regular use by a local occult group who were performing rituals in the upper rooms, and had painted Aleister Crowley-inspired magical symbols on the floors and walls.

Ironically, these protagonists confirm today that the house certainly was haunted – but not by them. They remember the sound of footsteps and weird bangings when they were alone in the house, an overbearing sense of being watched, and a presence on the stairs. One recalls hearing, in the company of an American student of the occult named Debbie, the disturbed sighing of a woman approaching via the stairs and echoing around the room after their associates had vacated for the evening. Other sounds which the pair heard after their rituals included what appeared to be deliberate knocking sounds from the lower parts of the house.

The house's haunted reputation certainly pre-dates 1973, however.

One then resident of nearby Williams Close, John Duffy, remembers spending time in the house as a 4-year-old when he was babysat by a Mrs Murphy, the house's then owner. As he recalls, 'I always felt uneasy in that house; it had a bad feel about it.' After the fire, he returned to the house with his friend 'Clarky', to dig up some plants. The pair separated, and as John was bent over in the soil, he jumped up upon hearing 'an almighty crash', and saw Clarky running away. When John tracked Clarky down, he learned that the cause of his flight was witnessing the large glass window at the back of the house 'explode from the inside'. Stephen Peacock, who was also a local teenager at the time, remembers

Number 1 Avenue Road, photographed by the Hornsey Journal in 1973. The black ring indicates the room where magical symbols were found painted on the walls.

What goes on at the 'House of Dracula'?

SCHOOLCHILDREN have nick-named this derelict neo-gothic mansion "the House of Dracula." It stands at the junction of Crescent Road and Avenue Road, Crouch End.

Neighbours talk of strange goings-on at night and mysterious noises and flickering lights in upper windows.

Article in the Hornsey Journal, *1973.*

exploring the house in the mid-1970s with a group of friends. One of these hurtled down the stairs and out of the house, convinced that 'something' on the stairs was chasing him. No present-day hauntings at Number 1 Avenue Road, which is now occupied by a sheltered housing complex, have been reported. Perhaps the ghosts that wandered the old house's corridors so long ago were dispersed by the wrecking ball amongst the brick dust, and finally set free.

The Hornsey Coal Ghost of Ferrestone Road

Concluding our journey across Highgate, we come to the ancient church tower of St Mary's, Hornsey. It is in the vicinity of this tower that one of the most extreme poltergeist outbreaks of the twentieth century was recorded. Until Highgate became a parish in its own right in 1898, this was the official place of worship for residents of Highgate. Early sources indicate that the tower was constructed from heavy slabs of stone and ironstone rubble taken from the abandoned lodge on the other side of Highgate Village, where black masses had been said some sixty years earlier in an attempt to end the life of the then 'boy king'. These rough-hewn blocks can still be seen supporting the upper part of the tower. This was added in 1832, when the decayed medieval nave and chancel were rebuilt. Perhaps the parish's choice of building materials was unwise, for St Mary's never appears to have experienced good fortune, and less than a century later this 'new' church was also demolished, with the exception of the tower.

A damp and uninhabitable rectory, which was frequently left abandoned by absentee vicars, stood nearby, and its substantial 'glebe land' was sold for housing development in 1883. By the early 1900s Ferrestone Road, a short terrace of four-storeyed houses, had been erected. The small gardens of these smart dwellings back on to the old burial ground, and the back windows today command a rather romantic view of the rustic tower which stands just 40 yards to the north. The first inhabitants were soon to discover, however, that their freshly laid lawns – and the very foundations of their homes – harboured a gruesome secret. Probably to avoid the lengthy legal process of applying to the parish vestry for permission, it seems that the construction company which built Ferrestone Road omitted to remove the hundreds of bodies which lay in their way.

In those days, the grounds of St Mary's presented a far less cared-for aspect than can be enjoyed today. Despite an order of 1882 prohibiting fresh burials, these had continued until 1894, due to the added pressure for plots created by the poor of Highgate, who could ill-afford to be buried in Highgate Cemetery or the chapel of ease. This 'overcrowding' had serious consequences, and by 1895, the *Surrey Standard* reported that the churchyard's dilapidated state had 'become a nuisance to the neighbourhood, while a bank in the western part of the ground [had] crumbled away so as to reveal some of the coffins in the vaults.' Regular flooding, caused by the New River, forced coffins and ancient tombstones to rise up out of the earth, and these, along with long-since forgotten entrances to underground crypts, continue periodically to reveal themselves in the gardens of Ferrestone Road to this day.

Writing as late as 1951, R.J. Cruikshank in *The Moods of London* described this corner of the capital as 'dank and dripping' when recalling his 1921 visit to this 'dejected street, in the winter dusk'. He immediately found the place eerie, and a suitable home for the 'poltergeist' which he had been invited to meet.

This malevolent 'entity' is little spoken of today, despite holding the unusual distinction of having allegedly caused the death of the youngest child of the family it was tormenting. The events in question

View from St Mary's Hornsey of Ferrestone Road, showing the chaotic graveyard which continues into the back gardens. (© Dave Milner)

commenced on New Year's Day 1921. At this time, a house in Ferrestone Road was occupied by a family by the name of Frost. It has since been converted into four flats, but in January 1921 it consisted of a basement with a coal cellar and kitchen, a first-floor drawing room and dining room, a second floor with two bedrooms, and two further attic sleeping areas. Within this narrow house dwelt the sole bread-winner, Mr Ivan Frost, his octogenarian parents, his wife, and their two adult sons. Three recent additions to the household were the children of Ivan's sister, Gordon aged 11, Bertie aged 9, and Muriel aged 5, their mother having died in the house from tuberculosis the previous April.

On 1 January 1921, the Frosts were alarmed when their regular order of coal began to spit and hiss in the cellar, despite not having being lit. When moved into the drawing room, the coals leapt from the scuttle, and from the cold grates. Mr Frost, concerned that some explosive material had contaminated the coal, contacted the police and the local fire brigade. To his dismay, despite both authorities witnessing the 'dancing coal' leaping from their own hands, no logical explanation was afforded. Subsequently, Mr Frost removed all of the coal to the back garden. It returned. According to Mr Frost, who by now was considering that these events might have a supernatural causation, whatever negative energy was afflicting his home seemed to be 'rising up through the house'. Loud bangs in the night betrayed the movement of lumps of the rejected coal heading up the staircase and bouncing upon the upper landings.

Other strange events followed, initially focused around the basement kitchen; knocks were heard at the windows, some of which were inexplicably smashed, and cutlery, crockery and cheese were thrown about. Ivan Frost reported that one morning at breakfast the mahogany kitchen table floated upwards of its own volition, while the seated Gordon was seen to levitate 2 feet into the air in his chair, before he fell and hurt himself. The chair continued to rise upwards until it met the ceiling, before crashing to the floor. After Mrs Frost Snr attempted to communicate with the unseen force by the use of rappings, the happenings seem to have increased dramatically.

The two young boys complained of being visited at night by a 'lady dressed in red'. This shade, which frightened the boys, claimed to be their deceased mother, who had come to 'take them with her'. The boys' grandmother was convinced that whatever the boys witnessed was not her daughter. Soon other parts of the house were affected, and objects including a pin cushion, a pack of playing cards, brooms, candlesticks, towels, a flat iron and plant pots were seen to rotate and fly about the rooms. Some objects, such as a valuable mantle clock, simply vanished for good.

Ferrestone Road quickly made national headlines. One journalist reported fighting his way through a throng of spectators, in order to interview Mr Frost's wife, to find that 'the blinds were drawn, and all the china had been removed from the mantle shelf to prevent the unknown agency from committing further depredations'. The nervous and visibly strained Mrs Frost described being awoken in the night by a loud thud, whilst sharing a bed with Bertie and Muriel. When her son rushed in, he found an orange in the bed, along with a shoe

The remains of St Mary's church tower, Hornsey. (© Dave Milner)

and a chair which had been hurled at them. A terrified Muriel confirmed that the orange had been repeatedly thrown against her head. Around this time, like Gordon, the diminutive Muriel was also observed to have been violently thrown

upwards into the air along with the chair she was seated upon.

The same journalist recalled hearing bangs from the kitchen, and rushing down to find Mrs Frost Snr seated with Muriel and Gordon at the table. A loaf of

Newspaper article about the Ferrestone Road poltergeist from the Courier, 21 February 1921.

bread had just floated from the kitchen table into an open drawer, and the bread board had been thrown to the floor. Perhaps most disturbingly, the bread knife had seconds previously hurtled past Gordon's ear and lodged itself in the wall.

The children's nerves rapidly became frayed. Gordon began to exhibit tremors whilst falling asleep, after which his body temperature would drop dramatically, and he was eventually admitted to Lewisham hospital suffering from a 'nervous collapse'. Gordon fled Ferrestone Road for good as soon as he was of legal age, but his little sister Muriel was denied this opportunity. On 31 March she passed away, aged just 5 years old. According to her uncle Ivan's official statement to the *Daily Mail* on 1 April 1921:

> Muriel took all the phenomena with calmness until a week or so ago. But since a bedstead rose, knocking over a chair and causing her to fall and bite her tongue, she has been much scared. Just before her death the house became a mass of rappings. Early this week she was taken suddenly ill, and died on Thursday morning. We are all convinced that she has been worried into this illness.

The Society for Psychical Research, which investigated this case on 18 February 1921, was reluctant to concede any paranormal origins to poltergeist cases involving children until the 1980s. By the early 2000s a relatively popular consensus had evolved within the paranormal community that in some cases there exists some as yet undefined energetic connection between poltergeist activity and children approaching or going through adolescence who are resident in the afflicted household. While the validity of this theory appears to hold weight in many cases, the concept that 'disturbed' teenagers can be held responsible for the subconscious moving of objects, and other acts that are attributed to poltergeists, is now so commonplace that it often overshadows other less-explored but equally valid hypotheses for unexplained phenomena. The SPR's early approach tended to ignore the potential psychic influence of young people upon the physical realm altogether, and attributed most poltergeist activity to children's pranks. This may explain why their 1915 report about similar disturbances at 'a haunted house in Hornsey, not far removed from an old priory', where 'tapping, crashes and other sinister noises' were heard, along with 'ornaments knocked from the mantelpiece', and 'a shut knife [being] snatched from a child's hand found with the open blade buried in the doorway' was never archived. The unspecified location of this haunting could be either Ferrestone Road itself or, more likely, one of the handful of roads which lay between it and nearby Priory Park. With hindsight this omission leaves us with the unsettling suggestion that the events mirrored a similar case which took place very nearby, some six years earlier. The similarities also invite us to question whether whatever aggressive force was behind the Ferrestone Road incidents was operating far beyond the energetic influence of two troubled young boys.

When interviewed in 1999, Pauline, the current owner of the house, reported that even on blisteringly hot summer afternoons certain areas in the house were intensely cold, especially in the remains of the old Victorian kitchen. Pauline also recalled witnessing a column of smoke rising up through the floor in the living room, and 'imploding'. One is left to wonder whether Mr Frost's intuition that the dark forces invading the house were rising up from its foundations, was correct.

6

SOME ANIMAL GHOSTS

We have already seen how several dogs have allegedly reacted to paranormal activity in Swains Lane. But what are we to make of Highgate's animal ghosts? For not all spectres which make their presence felt in Highgate are humanoid in appearance. While a few witnesses claim to have seen phantom cats and dogs in both sides of the cemetery, fortunately no hellhounds have been reported (so far). Indeed, the most detailed reports which comprise the village's supernatural bestiary point to ghostly fauna of a somewhat domestic nature.

An Invisible Horse and Rider in Swains Lane

We will probably never know what potentially paranormal occurrences are parodied in *Gambado on Horsemanship* of 1808 (see Chapter 1). But perhaps we find a clue in two reports of ethereal riders on horseback recorded some two centuries later.

Caroline Murray, producer of *Dark Journey* (2012), a horror film set and filmed on location around Highgate and Hampstead, recalled to this author an unsettling group experience which occurred one night in October 2010. During the pre-production stages of the film, Caroline, James White (the film's director) and a Canadian friend of James were visiting potential 'haunted' locations which could provide backdrops for their film. One October evening the team found themselves wandering down Swains Lane, shortly after midnight. It was an exceptionally cold and windy night, and unsurprisingly the area was deserted, with not even a passing car to dispel the silence and deep sense of isolation. Not put off, the team continued taking test shots through the cemetery railings, and up and down the lane, for half an hour or so. It was around this time that all three began to hear what sounded like the distant noise of horses' hooves, cantering down the lane. At first the sound seemed to come from a couple of hundred yards away, but it quickly grew closer.

The noise of phantom hoof beats increased until it was virtually upon the three adventurers, at which point all present felt a sudden gust of wind, and heard a swift rushing sound, as if a horse and rider had galloped past them. This shared encounter unnerved the witnesses to such a degree that, after many subsequent conversations about what happened that night, they decided to incorporate it into their film. This resulted in a nightmare sequence, where the lead character, 'Kelly', runs down Swains Lane accompanied by the clamour of pursuing horses.

Unbeknown to the *Dark Journey* production team, in the mid-1990s a Canadian music producer, who, for reasons which will become obvious, wishes to be referred to only by his first name, had a similar experience in the lane. 'Mike' was at that time the occupant of 85 Swains Lane, a concrete, glass and steel building designed by the architect John Winter to complement his own 'Modern House' slightly further down the lane. Like the rest of the domiciles on this small stretch of track, Mike's back door opened directly on to Highgate Cemetery West. In the mid-1990s, heavily involved with London's goth scene, Mike converted much of 85 Swains Lane into a recording studio, which quickly became a hangout for people of an alternative bent. Inspired by the expansive views of the cemetery from Mike's living room, a small group of his acquaintances devised a plot for a music video, which, with the ease of access afforded by Mike's property, was proposed to be filmed in the Circle of Lebanon. The inevitable police presence which this would attract was incorporated into the storyboard, with the participants planning to 'disappear' through Mike's backdoor into the unlit house, thus avoiding detection.

This scheme was never to materialise, however. Returning home up Swains Lane late one winter's night, Mike was alarmed to hear the distinct sound of a horse approaching at quite some speed. With a clear view up the empty lane, and with no horse corporeal or otherwise in sight, Mike ran as fast as he could towards his house and quickly locked the door behind him. Convinced that he had been 'warned off' by some supernatural agency, Mike dropped all plans to facilitate this project, and returned to Canada soon afterwards.

A Phantom Coach and Six

More equine phantoms are alluded to by the author of 'A Few Ghosts for Christmas-time'. This article appeared in the *New Monthly Magazine and Literary Journal*, December 1829, and informs its readers that:

> They who think that the public are getting too wise for their superstitions, and that gas-light and steam-engines are beginning to frighten the ghosts themselves, will be glad to hear that there is a spectre no farther from town than Highgate. It haunts the lane between Highgate and Hampstead, leading from the Gate-house to the agreeable inn called the Spaniards; and appears in the shape of a coach-and-six.

The Frozen Chicken of Pond Square

If this ethereal coach was still journeying about Highgate by 1943, it may be the same as that heard by Aircraftman

Terrence Long some 100 yards to the south, on a cold December night that year. According to an article by reporter Leslie Thomas, published by the *London Evening News* in 1958, Long was crossing Pond Square, which was then entirely blacked out as per wartime regulations, when he heard 'hoof-beats, the sudden pulling up of a carriage, and then a frightened shriek'. Long stopped, 'his eyes trying vainly to pierce the darkness'. As the clouds parted, and the moon shone down upon the looming eighteenth-century townhouses, Long encountered 'the ghost'. 'It was a frightened, squawking fowl, dashing about in frenzied circles, half-running, half-flying – and shivering!' Thomas's piece alleges. After closing his eyes, and 'taking a deep lungful of the chill air', Aircraftman Long looked again to find that the mysterious bird had vanished.

Taking fright and running out of the square, Long collided with a fire-watcher, whom he initially took to be another ghost, on account of his shroud-like black cape. Without laughing, the night-watchman confirmed that Long's sighting of the ghostly chicken, which a breathless Long described as having hardly any feathers, was not unique. Indeed, he claimed that it had been witnessed for years. Despite not having seen the chicken himself, the fire-watcher recounted an occasion a month or two before, when:

> some of the people round here saw a man actually trying to catch it. He chased it all around the square – probably thought it would help his meat ration. It jumped and flew all over the place with this chap after him. THEN IT WENT STRAIGHT THROUGH A BRICK WALL!

Another witness cited by Thomas is a Mrs John Greenhill, who is disallowed her own first name in the article owing to the anachronistic convention, still practised into the 1950s, of identifying a woman by her husband's forename. Mrs Greenhill describes the chicken as 'a big, whitish bird, [which] used to perch on the lower boughs of the tree opposite our house'. She also volunteers that 'many members of my family have seen it on moonlit nights'.

Peter Underwood, in his previously discussed 1973 publication *Haunted London*, makes vague reference to two later sightings of the fowl in 1969 and 1970. As discussed in Chapter 2, many bizarre stories were circulating in Highgate around this time, and perhaps understandably, these were two of the least credible. Underwood also repeats what has now become almost a mantra in paranormal 'non-fiction' – the tale of Sir Francis Bacon and his supposed connection to the ghost of a 'frozen chicken'.

Since at least the publication of Thomas's article, the rumour that a mournful chicken haunts the square has been circulated in print and latterly (extensively) online. This folkloric tale always repeats the same loose plot, chiefly focused upon the death of the famous politician and philosopher Francis Bacon at Highgate, from pneumonia. Bacon's illness is alleged to have been instigated by a terrible cold, which he caught whilst conducting an early experiment regarding the potential of refrigeration, something that we now take for granted but which was then a new idea. This experiment is universally claimed to have involved stuffing a chicken with snow, taken from the banks of the frozen pond from which the square takes its name.

Pond Square. (© Dave Milner)

Suddenly taken sick, Bacon is then conveyed to the home of his friend Lord Arundel, where he passes away a few days later.

These asserted facts are all questionable, as we shall see, with the exception of Bacon's death occurring at the home of Lord Arundel. Arundel owned many properties in Highgate, but the most likely candidate for Bacon's deathbed scene is 'Old Hall' in South Grove, now the home of Terry Gilliam of Monty Python fame. Bacon's Lane, named for Bacon's association with the area, runs practically adjacent to the house to this day.

The many popular narratives which recount Bacon's death chiefly derive from two sources. The first is a letter which the dying Bacon wrote to Lord Arundel, thanking him in his absence for his hospitality. The second is John Aubrey's *Brief Lives*, a collection of manuscripts which its author began compiling in 1680. These fascinating tracts provide a plethora of obscure details pertaining to the careers, and private lives, of well-known public figures of the seventeenth century.

It is from Thomas Hobbes (1588–1679), a philosopher friend of Bacon's, that Aubrey allegedly gleaned the circumstances surrounding Bacon's fatal trip to Highgate in 1626. 'Mr Hobbs told me,' he writes:

that the cause of his Lordship's death was trying an Experiment; *viz.* as he was taking the aire in a Coach with Dr Witherborne (a Scotchman, Physitian to the King) towards High-gate, snow lay on the ground, and it came into my Lord's thoughts, why flesh might not be preserved in snow, as in Salt. They were resolved they would try the Experiment presently. They alighted out of the Coach and went into a poore woman's house at the bottom of Highgate hill, and bought a Hen, and made the woman exenterate it, and then stuffed the body with Snow, and my Lord did help to doe it himselfe. The Snow so chilled him that he imme-diately fell so extremely ill, that he could not returne to his Lodging (I suppose then at Graye's Inne) but went to the Earle of Arundel's house at High-gate, where they putt him into a good bed warmed with a Panne, but it was a damp bed that had not been layn-in in about a yeare before, which gave him such a colde that in 2 or 3 dayes as I remem-ber Mr Hobbes told me, he dyed of Suffocation.

Aubrey's account has been challenged, however, by scholars who point out that the only historical reference to a 'Dr Witherborne' is to be found in *Brief Lives*. The physician to James I at the time of Bacon's death was in real-ity the Englishman William Harvey (1578–1657). Additional doubt is thrown upon the legitimacy of Aubrey's nar-rative by the improbability that Bacon, with his vast education and knowledge of ancient history, was unaware of the practice of using harvested ice to con-serve foodstuffs by the ancient Romans, Chinese and Greeks.

Alan Stewart and Lisa Jardine, in their book *Hostage to Fortune: The Troubled Life of Francis Bacon* (1998), provide most illuminating suggestions about the real circumstances surrounding Bacon's death. After painstaking research, they conclude that there was in fact no 'snow on the ground' in the spring of 1626, and after contextually analysing the language used by Bacon in his letter to Arundel, they deduce that his death was far removed from any unwarranted exposure to icy weather. The authors suggest that Bacon's references to self-experimentation imply that it was not a chicken upon which he was testing fledgling scientific methods, but his own body. Specifically, based upon the historical allusions made in the letter about similar experiments, they con-clude that Bacon, then aged 65, died after inhaling opium or, more likely, potassium nitrate. This rash action may well have been an attempt to prolong his own life, which is supported by Aubrey's earlier explanation of how Bacon came to be in Highgate in the first place, namely that 'In April, and the Springtime, his Lordship would, when it rayned, take his Coach (open) to recieve the benefit of Irrigation, which he was wont to say was very wholsome because of the Nitre in the Aire.'

Fascinating as these deductions are in their own right, perhaps most significant of all is the fact that none of the hundreds of repetitive retellings of Bacon's last days take note of one simple statement made by Bacon himself. In his letter to Lord Arundel, Bacon clearly states that the experiment he had conducted was 'entirely successful', but that 'in the jour-ney *between* London and Highgate [my italics]' he became seriously ill with a fit of 'casting' (or vomiting). From this we can definitively conclude, from the most reliable source which it would be possible to obtain, that whatever Bacon's experiment was, it had already been concluded by the time he left London for Highgate. That Bacon had an upset stomach by the time he reached Highgate Hill makes it even less likely that he would have purchased food. If this *was* an alternative purpose for acquiring the chicken, it is rendered even more improbable by the many public houses then providing cooked meals in the vicinity.

A prudent reader may conclude that Bacon's demise had nothing whatever to do with an attempt to extend the shelf life of a freshly killed chicken. Which leaves us pondering what came first, the ghostly chicken or the rumour which has been claimed to explain its presence?

With the exception of Underwood's unnamed sources, whether the spectral fowl really exists at all seems to hinge largely upon the testimonies of the three witnesses referenced by Leslie Thomas.

Thomas claims that 'the residents, and some of their neighbours in that part of Highgate, have long known about the strange spectre'. During my many interviews with local residents I have been unable to locate even one who remembers an instance of the chicken's alleged manifestations. Nor have I been able to find any sources which support the oft-proposed idea that the ghost has been seen since Bacon's era (although one cannot discount the possibility that oral traditions pertaining both to wartime and earlier sightings continued until the end of the twentieth century).

The narrow passageway which leads from Pond Square to Highgate High Street. Could this be where the 'phantom' fowl made its escape? (© Dave Milner)

What residents do remember is the popularity amongst many Highgate villagers of keeping chickens to supplement wartime rationing. For decades foxes are known to have been breeding in nearby Highgate Cemetery, as well as Highgate and Queens Woods. It is quite possible that one such lupine burglar was disturbed by the torch of the fire-watcher whilst tearing open a chicken coop. This would easily explain a confused and partially featherless fowl, shivering with fear, and running in panicked circles in the square.

Living chickens are unknown to be able to run through brick walls. A narrow passageway, however, no more than a yard wide, which leads off Highgate High Street and down into Pond Square, perhaps lends a clue to the sudden disappearance of the chicken in the stygian lighting conditions of a wartime blackout.

Such a compromised chicken, like the pair of wallabies found in Highgate Cemetery in 2013, is unlikely to have survived long, however, after being freed from captivity. The fact that Mrs Greenhill and the fire-watcher attest to many sightings of the bird during the Second World War does lend itself, bizarre as it sounds, to the possibility that the frightened bird may have been a ghost chicken after all. Perhaps, though, it met its maker some 317 years after Bacon did.

Although fresh perspectives have cast doubt upon any role which the unfortunate demise of Francis Bacon may have played in the true origins of the phantom fowl, one nagging fact sullies what would otherwise be a tidy analysis of this much-circulated urban myth. The Dorking breed of chicken is one of the oldest known in England, having been introduced around the time of the Roman conquest. The oldest 'bloodline' known amongst what is now regarded as a heritage breed is that of the 'rose-combed white'. In contrast to the mass-rearing of brown-feathered hens today, this large white bird was the most common type of chicken bred for consumption in 1600s London.

'There are more things in heaven and earth …', to quote a hackneyed phrase, and perhaps, as we have seen, in Highgate anything is possible!

7

HAUNTED WOODS

From the mid-thirteenth century, vast tracts of terrain around Highgate were enclosed by hedgerows, demarking land owned by the bishops of London. This area was known as Hornsey Park, and contained hunting grounds, where wild boar were said to roam, and less wooded 'enparked' land, where deer and hares were nurtured. Today we can see the remains of this vast forest in the many pockets of woodland which have been preserved for public use. Popular among dog walkers and those seeking space to contemplate, these woods, however, are not always as peaceful as they might appear.

A Moonlit Pursuit in Cherry Tree Wood

I am grateful to author Neil Arnold for allowing me to reproduce the following account of a paranormal encounter in Cherry Tree Wood, which dates back to the mid-1980s. The witness, a Mr Lambert, recalls:

I was on my way home from an old girlfriend's house. It was late and the quickest way to the taxi office was a path through the middle of the woods. It was a full moon that night, and the air was thick and heavy. It was a very eerie night. It was very dark in the woods. The only light was that of the moon which sat low in the sky.

All of a sudden I felt the need to run, but I said to myself, 'Oh, you're just being silly', and carried on walking. But I started to feel uneasy, as if eyes were watching me from all around. Then I felt as if there was someone or something behind me. The hair on my neck started to stand on end and I heard a voice say: 'Run!' And I did run, all the way to the taxi office. I don't know why but I'm sure the presence I felt was very old and dark and meant me no harm. I recently returned to Cherry Tree Wood after twenty years. Even in daylight I feel that people are not the only things that dwell there. That night is one that will stay with me for the rest of my life.

Sensations of inexplicable panic and terror whilst walking alone through woods are widely reported. Some schools of thought propose logical explanations, such as disorientation and a fear of becoming lost. Others suggest that the now rare opportunity to connect with nature, especially in ancient woodland, can leave witnesses open to primal forces which can challenge the comfort and familiarity of the modern world. Before the development of Woodside Avenue, Cherry Tree Wood was a natural continuation of Highgate Wood's 69 acres, and here many more visual encounters with something seemingly old, and certainly unexplained, have been reported.

A Tall, Dark Figure Gliding between the Trees

Crouch End resident Chris Layden's 1991 experience in Highgate Wood is a typical (although chilling) example of these frequent sightings. Like most, it occurred near a 2,000-year-old beech tree, adjacent to the Roman settlement from around AD 200 which was discovered in 1962. This is one of the quieter and hillier areas of the wood, where one rarely meets another human being. Late one December afternoon Mr Layden was walking his dog, when the animal suddenly pulled on the leash, and began to whine. Glancing up, Mr Layden was astonished to see, a few yards away, a 'darkly draped figure' which appeared to be gliding along just above the ground.

'I have always kept an open mind to such things, but I know what I saw. It looked like the figure of a nun. Whatever it was appeared from nowhere, then glided for 30 feet or so before it just disappeared,' remembers Mr Layden.

Mr Layden was unable to discover any obvious cause for the phenomenon, although he did note a small cold spot by the oak tree near which the figure had vanished. An apparition of a nun has been reported at this location for decades, and it has been suggested that she was in life associated with a religious house which may have stood at the beginning of nearby Shepherds Hill. She could equally have been a member of the twelfth-century order of Our Lady of Muswell, which owned land near the top of Highgate Woods. Other witnesses have described seeing something similar, but with a more sinister demeanour and of greater proportions, suggesting that there may be at least two spectres roaming the woods. If this tall, dark figure has been appearing since the earliest occupation of the site, it is just possible that the Romans made an unsuccessful attempt to keep it out. Since the 1960s archaeologists have puzzled over the purpose of a large manmade earthwork which bisects the wood, just to the south of the abandoned Roman pottery ...

Woodland Sprites Coming in from the Cold?

Muswell Hill Road, once a narrow country lane, divides Highgate Wood and Queens Wood. Developed in the 1880s, and now lined with large Victorian houses, it is likely that this is the road referred to by local historian Dr Oliver Natelson in a 2005 interview:

The 2,000-year-old beech tree adjacent to the Roman settlement, which was discovered in Highgate Wood in 1962. Sightings of a gliding nun and a tall, dark figure have been reported in this vicinity. (© Dave Milner)

In the 1940s, a family, living near Highgate Wood, found dog biscuits arranged in a u-shape around the back of an armchair. The room had been locked and no-one had been there the night before. Puzzled, they put it down to a harmless prank, but were shocked when the same thing kept on happening. Pulling back the carpet, the owners sprinkled flour around the chair to catch out the trickster, but the next morning the biscuits were back and the flour undisturbed. In the 1990s, along the same road in Highgate, a frightened woman reported her bed shaking furiously, typical of a poltergeist presence.

A Plague Victim's Ghost in Queens Wood

Queens Wood was given its present name in honour of Queen Victoria, but since the seventeenth century it was known as Churchyard Bottom Wood. No church ever existed here, the name deriving from the mass plague pits which were dug in 1665, to accommodate the 'immense number of contagious corpses brought from the metropolis'. These long-forgotten hollows were rediscovered in the Victorian era, when 'at a few feet from the surface [were] found vast quantities of human bones, intermixed with darkened strata of earth' (Frederick Prickett, *The History and Antiquities of Highgate, Middlesex*, 1842).

It was near this spot, now covered by a children's play area, that George Curtis had a disturbing and extremely unusual experience at around 5 p.m. one October in 1975. Out walking with his father and their dog, George noticed something dark vibrating in mid-air just ahead of them. The dog seemed more curious than afraid, and as they stared at the object, it became clear that it was a rectangular shape, hovering at a 30- or 40-degree angle, and on it, arms crossed over his chest, appeared to be a man. As George shouted for his dad to turn and look at it, the figure melted away.

That some victims of bubonic plague were accidentally buried alive has been proposed by many historians. It is highly likely that, not wishing to catch the Black Death themselves, and anxious to offload their laden carts, those responsible for burying the afflicted did not perform thorough checks once the patient had slipped into a death-like coma. That whoever George saw being lowered into his grave may have been aware of what was happening, but unable to communicate, does not bear thinking about. We can only hope that what George witnessed was some kind of recording from the past, perhaps created by the trauma experienced by the 'undertaker' and not his charge.

The 'Mothman' of Queens Wood

Our final, and perhaps most terrifying, encounter in the woods comes from Brett Haines, then aged 19. One winter night in 1996, approaching 11 p.m., Brett was on his way from Crouch End to a friend's party in Highgate. In a rush, he decided to take the quickest route, which cuts through the lower end of Queens Wood. As he turned right into Queenswood Road, Brett suddenly stopped in his tracks. For, as he recalls, some 10 feet ahead of him and to the right of the path, something monstrous had stepped out from behind a tree:

It was about 7 feet tall, and it didn't have a face. All I could make out was some sort of black cloak, or bodysuit. To be honest, my first thought was 'why is Batman standing in Queens Wood?' Especially when it raised its arms, which seemed sort of webbed, in the way they came out from its torso. The whole thing happened so fast that I couldn't think straight. I wish it *had* been Batman, because this thing felt evil. I didn't know if it was going to fly up into the trees, or lunge at me. I don't know what it was, but it wasn't human, and it wasn't someone dressed up.

Brett turned and ran back to Wood Vale as fast as he could. He ran all the way up Shepherds Hill, and didn't stop running until he collapsed against his friend's door in Highgate. Too scared to glance over his shoulder, Brett never knew if the creature in Queens Wood followed him, and to this day has never set foot in the woods again.

The path through Queens Wood where, on a winter night in 1996, Brett Haines claims to have been terrified by a mothman-like creature, which stepped out from behind a tree. (© Dave Milner)

Also from The History Press

More Spooky Books

Printed in Great Britain
by Amazon

41750917R00066